MARX ON SUICIDE

EDITED AND WITH INTRODUCTIONS BY
ERIC A. PLAUT AND KEVIN ANDERSON

MARX

ON

SUICIDE

TRANSLATED BY

Eric A. Plaut, Gabrielle Edgcomb, and Kevin Anderson

NORTHWESTERN UNIVERSITY PRESS

Evanston, Illinois

Northwestern University Press
Evanston, Illinois 60208-4210

Printed in the United States of America
ISBN 0-8101-1632-4 (cloth)
ISBN 0-8101-1638-3 (paper)

Library of Congress Cataloging-in-Publication Data

Marx, Karl. 1818–1883.
    Marx on suicide / edited and with introductions by Eric A. Plaut
and Kevin Anderson ; translated by Eric A. Plaut, Gabrielle Edgcomb,
and Kevin Anderson.
        p.   cm. — (Pyschosocial issues)
    Karl Marx published an essay titled "Peuchet on suicide" based on
the writings of Jacques Peuchet, 1758–1830.
    Includes bibliographical references.
    ISBN 0-8101-1632-4 (cloth). — ISBN 0-8101-1638-3 (pbk.)
    1. Suicide.   2. Peuchet, J. (Jacques), 1758–1830.   I. Plaut, Eric
A. II. Anderson, Kevin, 1948–   . III. Title. IV. Series.
HV6545.M276   1999   99-19436
362.28—dc21   CIP

CONTENTS

I INTRODUCTION

Marx on Suicide in the Context of His Other Writings on Alienation and Gender

Kevin Anderson

T he text by Marx on suicide included in this volume is unusual in several respects. First, it is Marx's only published discussion of suicide. After he published this brief article in 1846 in *Gesellschaftsspiegel* (*Mirror of Society*), a small German socialist journal in which Engels was involved, he never returned to the topic. Second, this text contains one of the most sustained discussions of gender in Marx's early writings. Marx concentrates here on the suicide of women, linking these events to women's oppression inside the French bourgeois family. Of the four case studies he takes up in some detail in this text, three concern suicides by women. Third, the structure of this text is somewhat unusual. Published under the title "Peuchet: On Suicide," it is not, properly speaking, an article by Marx. It consists of Marx's brief four-paragraph introduction, followed by his edited translation of lengthy excerpts on suicide in early-nineteenth-century Paris drawn from the memoirs of Jacques Peuchet, a leading French police administrator, economist, and statistician.[1]

This text bears some resemblance to a number of other Marx texts, today considered quite important to an understanding of his overall work. These texts take a somewhat similar form, mainly excerpts from other authors rather than Marx's own words. They include the "Conspectus of Bakunin's *Statehood and Anarchy*" (1874–75), one of Marx's more extensive treatments of anarchism; the *Ethnological Notebooks* (1880–82), which deals with the social structures of tribal and other non-Western societies in the Americas, India, and Australia, especially with regard to gender relations; and the *Mathematical Manuscripts* (dates uncertain). Several dozen volumes of these excerpt notebooks, which contain notes and occasional commentary on other authors, have never been published in any language, and will eventually appear in the *Marx-Engels Gesamtausgabe* (*MEGA*).[2] However, Marx's article on Peuchet and suicide, unlike his excerpt notebooks, was written for publication.

On the Eve of "Peuchet on Suicide": Alienation, Humanism, and Gender in Marx's Early Writings, 1844–45

From 1845 to 1846, when Marx composed and published this text on suicide, he was living in Belgium, having been expelled from France in January 1845 for his political activities, and also facing prosecution in the Prussian courts if he returned to his homeland. A bit earlier, during his stay in Paris from October 1843 to January 1845, Marx began to study political economy intensively. In Paris, he wrote, in what is today known as the *Economic and Philosophical Manuscripts of 1844*, his first comprehensive treatment of the nature of capitalist society, of alienation, of socialism and communism, and of his own version of dialectics. These issues were to be central to his work for the rest of his life. As is well known, in the *1844 Manuscripts* Marx conceptualizes for the first time the alienation faced by the industrial proletariat. The workers, he writes, are alienated from the products of their labor, as capitalism produces "palaces" for the wealthy "but for the worker, hovels."[3] While the latter problem is as old as the pyramids, what was new under capitalism was the way in which the very process of labor had turned the worker "into a machine" (*MECW* 3, p. 273), depriving him or her of "free, conscious activity." The latter, according to Marx, is the "species character of human beings" (*MECW* 3, p. 276). Its denial creates alienation in all human relationships. Such a machinelike existence, found in its most extreme form in the capitalist factory, is an increasingly general social fact in bourgeois society.

In another part of the *1844 Manuscripts*, the "Critique of the Hegelian Dialectic," Marx argues that, in the *Phenomenology of Spirit*, Hegel develops a critique, "although still in alienated form—of whole spheres like Religion, the State, Civic Life, etc." (*MECW* 3, p. 322). Marx outlines, here at an abstract philosophical level, an alternative to the human objectification found under capitalism. In critiquing Hegel's idealistic dialectic, he develops a humanist perspective, evoking "the actual corporeal human being, standing on firm and well-rounded earth, inhaling and exhaling all natural forces."[4] In the same passage, Marx identifies his own position as "a thorough-going naturalism or humanism [which] distinguishes itself both from idealism and materialism, and is, at the same time, the truth uniting both" (*MECW* 3, p. 336). Here Marx counterposes his own framework, which is as much humanist and idealist as it is materialist, to the limited horizon of capitalism, which masks the exploitation and alienation of labor under a hyperrealism which, on the one hand, views the worker as a mere object and, on the other, sees the dominant classes of society as composed of "naturally" acquisitive individuals.

In the *1844 Manuscripts*, there is also a brief but little-discussed passage on gender relations, in a part entitled

"Private Property and Communism." Even Herbert Marcuse, who published a fine and detailed study of the *Manuscripts* as early as 1932, failed to mention this passage, which was taken up only later by feminist thinkers such as Simone de Beauvoir and Raya Dunayevskaya.[5] In it, Marx writes:

> The direct, natural, necessary relationship of human being [*Mensch*] to human being is the *relationship of man [Mann] to woman [Weib]*. . . . Therefore, on the basis of this relationship, we can judge the whole stage of development of the human being. From the character of this relationship it follows to what degree the *human being* has become and recognized himself or herself as a *species being*; a *human being*; the relationship of man to woman is the *most natural* relationship of human being to human being. Therefore, in it is revealed the degree to which the *natural* behavior of the human being has become human. (*MECW* 3, pp. 295–96)[6]

In this remarkable passage, Marx seems to give a greater emphasis to gender than even to class relations as a measure of human development. Dunayevskaya writes that in the *Manuscripts* as a whole, far from concentrating exclusively on alienated labor, "Marx extended the concept of Alienation to the Man/Woman relationship and to all life under capitalism."[7]

The Holy Family, written in fall 1844, was Marx's first joint publication with Engels.[8] In this book, published in early 1845, they emphasize again and again "that the general position of women in modern society is inhuman" (*MECW* 4, p. 195), also defending the early socialist and feminist Flora Tristan from attacks on her alleged "feminine dogmatism" (*MECW* 4, p. 20). Tristan, who died in 1844 without having met Marx or Engels, in 1843 began to publish *L'Union ouvrière*, in which she was the first to advocate a workers' international, a "universal union of working men and women." She refused to separate the emancipation of labor from that of women, arguing that "the most oppressed man can oppress someone, his wife; [woman] is the proletarian of even the proletarian."[9]

At another point in *The Holy Family*, Marx applauds the worldview of the Paris prostitute Fleur de Marie, a fictional character in *Les Mystères de Paris*, a moralistic novel by Eugène Sue. Sue was a popular member of the Parisian literary left, whose sentimental novels sold very widely.

In an interesting account of Paris during this period, which may have some bearing on Marx's decision to write the piece on suicide, Walter Benjamin, writing in the late 1930s, discusses suicides by workers in Paris in the 1840s:

> Around that time the idea of suicide became familiar to the working masses. "People are scrambling for copies of a lithograph depicting an English worker who is taking his life because he despairs of earning a livelihood. One worker even goes to Eugène Sue's apartment and hangs himself there. In his hand is a slip of paper with this note: 'I thought dying would be easier for me if I die under the roof of a man who stands up for us and loves us.'"[10] In 1841 Adolphe Boyer, a printer, published a small book entitled *De l'état des ouvriers et de son amélioration par l'organisation du travail*. It was a moderate presentation that sought to recruit the old corporations of itinerant journeymen which stuck to guild practices for the workers' associations. His work was unsuccessful. The author took his own life and in an open letter invited his companions in misfortune to follow suit.[11]

Surprisingly, Benjamin does not mention Marx's article on suicide in Paris, even though it was published in German in

1932. Nor does he note the presence of Flora Tristan among the socialist writers of the 1840s. These suicides of English and French workers may have been a factor in turning Marx to the topic. However, as noted above, Marx's focus in his article was different—the suicides of bourgeois women, most of them living under severe familial constraints.

In *The Holy Family*, Marx attacks repeatedly the way in which Sue portrays Fleur de Marie as a sinful woman in need of religious redemption, which she receives at the cost of becoming overwhelmingly guilty and unhappy. Marx quotes Fleur de Marie as she recounts having contemplated suicide: "More than once I looked over the embankment of the Seine; but then I would gaze at the flowers and the sun and say to myself: the river will always be there and I am not yet seventeen years old." Marx writes that, "contrary to Christian *repentance*," upon her release from prison, Fleur de Marie exhibited "a free and strong nature" which was "at once Stoic and Epicurean" (*MECW* 4, p. 169; here and elsewhere, emphasis is in the original unless indicated otherwise).

The Holy Family contains the first outline by Marx and Engels of a historical materialist perspective. It forms part of a critique of their former colleagues, the German Young Hegelians.[12] However, they also continue to stress human creativity and subjectivity:

> *History* does *nothing*, it "possesses *no* immense wealth," it "wages *no* battles." It is the *human being*, the real living human being who does all that, who possesses and fights. . . . [H]istory is *nothing but* the activity of the human being pursuing his or her aims." (*MECW* 4, p. 93)[13]

Marx's intellectual development in this period has been illuminated further by the recent publication of volume IV/3 of the *MEGA*. This volume includes his excerpt-notebooks of 1844 to 1847. In their introduction to this volume, the editors note that in part of these extensive notes on economic literature Marx writes, in early 1845: "Should private property exist? Should the family exist?"[14] This was shortly after he finished writing *The Holy Family.*

In the spring of 1845, Marx formulated the "Theses on Feuerbach," in which he once again spoke of the importance of idealism as well as materialism. In the first thesis, he writes that "the main shortcoming of all materialism up to now (including that of Feuerbach)" lay in a contemplative stance which grasped reality "not however as *sensuous human activity, praxis;* not subjectively." Marx then points to the continuing importance of idealism for a revolutionary outlook: "Hence the *active side* was developed abstractly in opposition to materialism by idealism" (*MECW* 5, p. 3). The eleventh and last thesis contained the well-known statement "Philosophers have *interpreted* the world in various ways; the point is to change it" (*MECW* 5, p. 5). Less noticed in discussions of the theses is the fact that in the fourth thesis Marx specifically attacks the existing form of the family, writing that "it must be destroyed in theory and in practice" (*MECW* 5, p. 4).[15] His reasons will be discussed later.

Marx, Peuchet, and Suicide

It was in the following months that Marx wrote and translated the piece on suicide. In a letter of 20 January 1845, Engels informed Marx that he and Moses Hess, a founder of "True Socialism," the first form in which French socialist ideas reached Germany, were soon to begin publishing "*Gesellschaftsspiegel,* a monthly in which we shall depict social *misère* and the bourgeois regime" (*MECW* 38, p. 16). Hess, who was to be the main editor of the new journal, had come to know Marx when they both wrote for the *Rhein-*

ische Zeitung, a liberal daily paper which appeared in 1842 to 1843 and on which Marx rose to editor. This was just before the paper was closed by the government. In the *1844 Essays,* Marx had generously termed Hess's writings among the only *"original* German works of substance" on socialist theory (*MECW* 3, p. 232), but this did not mean overall agreement with them. Marx later broke decisively with Hess, writing in 1848 in the *Communist Manifesto* that Hess and other True Socialists kept their social critiques at too abstract a level, forgetting the economic content of socialism. Additionally, Marx charged, the True Socialists, operating in feudal-absolutist Germany, posed their critiques of the rising bourgeoisie in such a way as to give the Prussian state "a weapon for fighting the bourgeoisie" (*MECW* 6, p. 512). In their "anathemas" against "liberalism," he wrote, the True Socialists failed to remember that the socialist critique presupposed the victory of the bourgeoisie over absolutism and feudalism, and the existence of "representative government" as well as "bourgeois liberty and equality" (*MECW* 6, p. 511).[16]

In January 1845, Engels coauthored with Hess a statement of purpose for *Gesellschaftsspiegel.* Although it began with a somewhat sentimental Hess-oriented evocation of "the noble striving to hasten to the aid of suffering humanity," the bulk of the statement called for empirical, even "statistical" descriptions of social reality (*MECW* 4, p. 671). During that year, without giving up the dialectic or the humanist perspective elaborated in 1844, Marx was moving toward a more empirically grounded investigation of the real social and economic conditions of modern society as he continued his intensive studies of economics. In the spring of 1845, Engels' detailed study of the horrific conditions of mid-nineteenth-century working-class life, *The Condition of the Working Class in England,* was published in Germany. Excerpts of it were also printed in *Gesellschaftsspiegel.* By 1846, however, after only twelve issues had appeared, *Gesellschaftsspiegel* was shut down by the Prussian government.

Marx's text on Peuchet and suicide, written in late 1845,[17] was probably part of an effort to move German socialists toward a more concrete discussion of economic and social issues. Philippe Bourrinet, editor of the recent French edition of Marx's text, argues that it may have been intended as a veiled critique of the True Socialist editors of *Gesellschaftsspiegel.* Bourrinet writes that Marx here seemed to suggest that "writers like Peuchet, 'functionaries and practical bourgeois,' went beyond these would-be 'socialists' and 'communists' as a result of their real knowledge of social life."[18]

Jacques Peuchet (1758–1830) began his career as an economist, helping to compile a dictionary of trade in 1785, in which period he is generally credited with having coined the term "bureaucracy." During the early revolutionary years, 1789–1791, Peuchet held a post in police administration, but his moderate royalist views caused him to be arrested in 1792. He was soon released but lived in obscurity until 1801, when he was named to the first of a series of high economic and police posts under the Bonaparte regime. Peuchet's *Elementary Statistics of France* appeared in 1805, the year he also began working as a legal archivist. In 1815, under the Restoration, he retained a high-level position, now working with the Paris police archives. Peuchet's 1824 book on the early revolutionary leader Mirabeau, judged in the political climate of the day to be too favorable to the Revolution, caused his final dismissal the following year. However, Peuchet took with him into retirement extensive materials from the police archives.

Peuchet's name is little cited today, but his multivolume *Memoirs from the Police Archives* caused a sensation when it was published in 1838, eight years after his death. Besides Marx, another prominent nineteenth-century figure who was impressed by Peuchet was Alexandre Dumas, who drew the outline of *The Count of Monte-Cristo* (1844) from an episode in Peuchet's *Memoirs*.[19] Historians today are dubious as to the factual accuracy of Peuchet's text, but this question is difficult to resolve conclusively, since Peuchet did not reveal actual names and dates, apparently to protect the innocent from scandal. Another problem with verifying his accounts is that the Paris police archives were destroyed by fire during the Paris Commune of 1871.

In the brief introduction to his translation of Peuchet, Marx argues for the "superiority" of French writers over even English ones for "critical descriptions of social conditions." In this regard, he points to the work of French utopian socialist Charles Fourier but adds that important critiques of bourgeois society can be found not only in works by French socialist writers but also in those by bourgeois ones like Peuchet. Marx also makes the point that the excerpts from Peuchet, which he has translated, will show his German readers that it is not only the workers, but the whole of bourgeois society, that suffers under dehumanized social relations: "[I]t may show the extent to which it is the conceit of the benevolent bourgeoisie that the only issues are providing some bread and some education to the proletariat, as if only the workers suffer from present social conditions but that, in general, this is the best of all possible worlds" (see "Peuchet on Suicide," p. 45).[20] Here Marx's revolutionary humanism from 1844 shines forth, as he mocks the notion that human emancipation would consist of raising the working class to the level of those latter-day bourgeois Candides who are naively satisfied with their lot. Instead, Marx focuses on a total transformation of human relations, including the abolition of social classes altogether, the overcoming of alienated labor, and the critique of the family as yet another form of oppression.

Marx begins his selection from the chapter of Peuchet's *Memoirs* entitled "Of Suicide and Its Causes"[21] with the latter's critique of modern society as a whole: "The yearly toll of suicides, which is to some extent normal and periodic, has to be viewed as a symptom of the deficient organization of our society" (see p. 47). Marx not only translates, but, as elsewhere on occasion in his translation, he bends Peuchet's text a bit, here changing Peuchet's phrase "fundamental defect" to "deficient organization" and thereby making the critique more social and less moralistic.[22] At another point, without indicating that he has done so, Marx adds a phrase of his own, writing that "short of a total reform of the organization of our current society," any attempt to lower the suicide rate "would be in vain" (see p. 50). In another passage, this time translated without emendation by Marx, Peuchet offers Marx ammunition for his radical critique of the family when he writes that "the revolution did not topple all tyrannies," since tyranny continues to exist "in families, where it causes crises, analogous to those of revolutions" (see pp. 50–51).

In these excerpts from Peuchet's chapter, Marx gives most of the space to four detailed accounts of suicide, the first three of them by young women. In the first case, a young woman, the daughter of a tailor, loses her virginity when she spends the night at the home of her fiancé's family. After her parents discover the situation the next morning, they furiously berate her, also publicly humiliating her in front of the whole neighborhood. Soon after, she drowns herself in the Seine. In the middle of his translation, Marx adds his own critique of the authoritarianism of the bourgeois family: "Those who are most cowardly, who are least capable of resistance themselves, become unyielding as soon as they can exert absolute parental authority. The abuse of that authority also serves as a cruel substitute for all the submissiveness and depen-

dency people in bourgeois society acquiesce in, willingly
or unwillingly."[23]

The second case Marx translates involves spousal abuse
rather than parental tyranny, this time within a mixed-race
Martiniquan family. A well-to-do and extremely jealous husband, himself suffering from severe mental illness and physical deformity, keeps his young wife under lock and key. He
constantly accuses her of infidelity, subjects her to tirades
and other forms of verbal abuse, and forces himself on her
sexually. Before the husband's sympathetic brother and his
physician friends can intervene, the young woman drowns
herself in the Seine. Marx, in his remarks in the middle of the
translation of this story, attacks the notion of the wife as the
marital property of the husband, comparing it to slavery:

> The unfortunate woman was condemned to unbearable
> slavery and M. de M. exercised his slaveholding rights,
> supported by the civil code and the right of property.
> These were based on social conditions which deem love
> to be unrelated to the spontaneous feelings of the
> lovers, but which permit the jealous husband to fetter
> his wife in chains, like a miser with his hoard of gold,
> for she is but a part of his inventory. (See pp. 57–58.)

In the third case, the central issue is abortion rights. An
eighteen-year-old woman, pregnant from an affair with her
aunt's husband, a prominent banker, approaches a doctor on
the street, indicating that she will commit suicide if she
cannot obtain an abortion. The doctor refuses to become
involved, but later blames himself after the woman drowns
herself. In the fourth case, which is recounted more briefly,
the core issue is sudden unemployment. A member of the
royal guards loses his job one day without warning as a
result of cutbacks. Unable to find another job, and with his
family reduced to poverty and sliding into disaster, he kills
himself rather than live on as a "burden" to them.

Finally, to end his excerpts from Peuchet, Marx reproduces the latter's table analyzing suicides in Paris in 1824. These data are similar to those presented by Émile Durkheim in his *Suicide* (1897),[24] in that Peuchet's table shows almost twice as many suicides by men as by women and also a greater absolute number of suicides by unmarried than by married people. However, Marx does not comment on these data, nor on the fact that, following Peuchet, he has singled out female suicide rather than the more prevalent type of suicide, that by males.

Gender and the Family in Marx's Subsequent Writings

As far as I am aware, Marx never returned to the subject of suicide after 1845. He did, however, continue to develop the themes on gender and the family found in the text on Peuchet and suicide. Below, I will touch briefly on some examples.[25]

In *The German Ideology*, written between 1845 and 1846, Marx and Engels refer to the sexual division of labor as the original form of that division (*MECW* 5, p. 44). In 1848, in the *Communist Manifesto*, Marx calls for the "abolition [*Aufhebung*] of the family,"[26] adding:

The bourgeois clap-trap about the family and education, about the hallowed co-relation of parent and child, becomes all the more disgusting, the more, by the action of modern industry, all family ties among the proletarians are torn asunder, and their children transformed into simple articles of commerce and instruments of labor. (*MECW* 6, pp. 501–2)

Here the radicalism of Marx's attack on the bourgeois family seems to echo his 1845 text on suicide.

It is interesting to note that, as against Engels' earlier draft material for the *Manifesto*, little of which was used in the final version, the language on the family was considerably sharpened here by Marx. For example, the June 1847 "Draft of a Communist 'Confession of Faith,'" a document Engels wrote and got approved during a Communist League meeting which Marx did not attend, stated: "We will only interfere in the personal relationship between men and women or with the family in general to the extent that the maintenance of the existing institution would disturb the new social order" (*MECW* 6, p. 102).[27]

A decade later, Marx once again addresses the oppression of non-working class women in his 1858 article "Imprisonment of Lady Bulwer-Lytton," published in the *New York Tribune* (*MECW* 15, pp. 596–601). Here, Marx castigates Lord Edward Bulwer-Lytton, a prominent Tory leader, for having conspired to have Lady Rosina Bulwer-Lytton committed to an asylum. Rosina Bulwer-Lytton's supposedly irrational actions included her attempt to rent a meeting hall to give a political speech, in which she intended to express views contrary to those of her husband. Marx expresses particular outrage at the fact that their son Robert refused to support his mother and in fact assisted his father in what Marx evidently regarded as a patriarchal cabal.

Though there is no chapter specifically devoted to gender and the family in *Capital*, volume 1, first published in 1867, Marx argues in one passage, as he had in the *Manifesto*, that capitalism undermines the family among the working classes. Here, in the chapter "Machinery and Large Scale Industry," he adds that this process, which throws women and children into paid employment

> outside the sphere of domestic economy . . . does nevertheless create a new economic foundation for a higher form of the family and of relations between the sexes. It is of course just as absurd to regard the Christian Germanic form of the family as absolute and final

> as it would have been in the case of the ancient
> Roman, the ancient Greek, or the Oriental forms. . . .
> It is also obvious that the fact that the collective
> working group is composed of individuals of both
> sexes and all ages must under the appropriate condi-
> tions turn into a source of humane development,
> although in its spontaneously developed, brutal, capi-
> talist form, the system works in the opposite direc-
> tion.[28]

This evocation of a "higher form of the family and of relations between the sexes" would seem to flesh out a bit his
earlier call for "abolition" of the family, at least in its existing bourgeois form. It also shows that for Marx there are
many possible forms of the family, depending on the state
of economic and social development at any given time. One
constant, however, is Marx's opposition to all forms of the
patriarchal family and his support for women's liberation.

Marx's little-known and belatedly published *Ethnological Notebooks* contains his most extensive treatment of
gender and the family. A set of excerpt-notebooks composed between in 1880 and 1882, just before his death, this
text comprises notes on Lewis Henry Morgan and other
anthropologists. At one point in his notes on Morgan, Marx
quotes the former on the oppression of women in ancient
Greece: "From first to last among the Greeks a principle of
studied selfishness among the males, tending to lessen the
appreciation of women, *scarcely found among savages*. The
usages of centuries stamped upon the mind of Grecian
women a sense of their inferiority."[29] Apparently dissatis-
fied with such a one-sided view, which would tend to deny
the possibility of women's (or men's) seeing beyond patriarchy,[30] Marx comments: "But the situation of the god-
desses on Olympus demonstrates nostalgia for the former
and more free & influential position of the females."[31]

In 1884, shortly after Marx's death, Engels published, on the basis of Marx's notes and his own reading of Morgan, the well-known book *The Origin of the Family, Private Property, and the State*. However, Engels saw a very close affinity not only between Marx and Morgan but also between the rise of private property and that of patriarchy. He also drew an idyllic, almost Rousseauian portrait of the primitive communalism of tribal societies. Dunayevskaya suggests that, contra Engels, "Marx demonstrated that, long before the dissolution of the primitive commune, there emerged the question of ranks *within* the egalitarian commune. . . . That is to say, within the egalitarian communal form arose the elements of its opposite—caste, aristocracy, and different material interests."[32] In these and other ways, Engels may have missed the subtlety of Marx's dialectical analysis.

As we have seen, Marx devoted substantial attention to gender and the family in the 1840s, when he formulated his overall concept of dialectics and of historical materialism. It is in this period that we can locate the text on suicide. He returned to these issues in a major way in the 1880s, at the close of his life, in the *Ethnological Notebooks*.

Marx and Durkheim on Suicide, Gender, and the Family

It may be unfair to discuss Marx's brief article and translation on suicide alongside Durkheim's 1897 masterwork, *Suicide: A Study in Sociology*. However, I do not think such a discussion is unwarranted, as will be shown below. First, let us review briefly some of the best-known features of Durkheim's study.

Durkheim discusses four main types of suicide.[33] (1) Egoistic suicide is a result of the rise of modern individualism and "varies inversely with the degree of integration of the social groups of which the individual is a part."[34] Modern society, which is poisoned by what Durkheim terms "excessive individualism" (p. 210), has witnessed an increase in the suicide rate. Exceptions to this occur during wars and revolutions, when there is greater than normal social solidarity. He points to the higher suicide rates among Protestants, who have greater individual independence than Catholics in working out their religious duties and beliefs, and among widowed men, who are socially isolated. (2) Closely related, anomic suicide is a product of the increasing anomie or normlessness of modern society. It, he writes, "results from man's activity lacking regulation and his consequent sufferings" (p. 250). Anomie in modern society also takes the form of "disturbances of the social equilibrium" (p. 246). As examples, Durkheim cites people who have suddenly gained wealth or been thrown into poverty by economic fluctuations and, once again, divorced men. Divorced women, in contrast, seem to enjoy some protection against suicide from their status. (3) If egoistic and anomic suicide are increasing as a result of modernization, another form, altruistic suicide, is becoming rarer. This form of suicide is caused not by excessive individualism but by a too weakly developed individuality. As examples, Durkheim cites *sati*, or widow suicide, in traditional India and other cases from non-Western and early societies. He also points to the relatively high rate of suicide among military officers in the industrialized countries as a more current, if receding, example. (4) A final form, fatalistic suicide, stemming from "excessive regulation," is relegated to a brief footnote (p. 276), apparently because this form, as exemplified by the suicide of slaves, was no longer important by 1897.

Certain similarities between the treatment of suicide by Marx and that by Durkheim are fairly obvious. Both Marx and Durkheim discuss suicide in modern society more in social than in psychological terms, both view suicide as symptomatic of broader social ills, and both are interested in empirical data on suicide rather than moral or philosophical speculation.

On the whole, however, the differences between the two discussions are more interesting and would seem to outweigh the similarities between Marx and Durkheim on suicide. One set of differences is methodological. Durkheim writes in his preface, here sounding rather positivist, that with regard to suicide, "real laws are discoverable which demonstrate the possibility of sociology better than any dialectical argument" (p. 37), adding that "sociology can and must be objective," and suggesting "the biologist" as a model for the social scientist (p. 39). Marx, while also drawing on a mass of empirical data in works such as *Capital*, continues to refer as well to the underlying dialectical method, inherited from Hegel, which structures his work.[35] A number of other differences between Marx and Durkheim emerge from an examination of how gender comes into play in Durkheim's *Suicide*, the subject of much recent discussion by sociologists.[36]

At several points in *Suicide*, Durkheim makes extremely disparaging comments about women, writing at one point that women's "mental life is less developed" than men's because "women's needs are more closely related to the organism" (p. 272). Terry Kandal attributes such statements to "the functionalism of the intellectual tradition that Durkheim had inherited."[37] No comparable statements can be found in Marx's work.

There is also the question of what Philippe Besnard has called the "incomplete [*inachevé*]" nature of Durkheim's *Suicide* with respect to women. Part of this problem, he writes, can be seen in Durkheim's very brief description of fatalistic suicide. This, Durkheim writes, is, as we have seen, "the suicide deriving from excessive regulation." Durkheim adds that this form involves "persons with futures pitilessly blocked and passions violently choked by oppressive discipline." In this regard, he briefly alludes to the suicide of "the married woman who is childless" as well as that of slaves, but he does not elaborate. However, he concludes, fatalistic suicide has "little contemporary importance" (p. 276). Despite the fact that he character- izes another form, altruistic suicide, deriving from a lack of individuality, as also very rare in modern Western soci- ety, Durkheim devotes an entire chapter to it, something Besnard calls "a surprising disproportionality."[38] This is all the more surprising, given the chapter "Of Suicide and Its Causes" in Peuchet's well-known *Memoirs*, a text with which Durkheim would possibly have been familiar.[39] In that chapter, Peuchet emphasizes (as did Marx in his arti- cle and translation) a type of suicide that was closer to Durkheim's fatalistic suicide than any of the other forms he puts forward—egoistic, anomic, and altruistic—and which he analyzes at such length. Most of the examples of suicide that Marx draws from Peuchet could be linked to the core issue in Durkheim's fatalistic suicide, excessive regulation. And they involve the suicide of women, an issue that Durkheim deemphasizes. The social ills that might lead to fatalistic suicide seemed to have far more contemporary relevance for Marx than for Durkheim. The last example Marx uses from Peuchet, however, on suicide and sudden unemployment, would fit more easily into Durkheim's category of anomic suicide, which derives from sudden changes in an individual's personal or eco- nomic life.

Finally, there is Durkheim's treatment of suicide and divorce, where he reports, on the basis of a lengthy statisti- cal analysis, that male suicide increases where divorce is less restricted, while that of females decreases under the same circumstances. Then, in his policy recommendations at the end of *Suicide*, Durkheim opposes liberalization of divorce, arguing instead for the strengthening of marriage. Because divorce or "conjugal anomie" is a major form of anomie, which is itself a major cause of male suicide, he recommends making "marriage more indissoluble." Durkheim acknowledges "that the suicides of husbands cannot be diminished in this way without increasing those of wives," but he seems, however reluctantly, to accept this as a necessary evil. He even asks: "Must one of the sexes necessarily be sacrificed?" (p. 384). Durkheim immediately tries to amend this rather jarring proposal, arguing that if women would take a more active role in society, the increase in female suicide due to marriage would lessen. However, he does not advocate greater equality for women, quickly inserting the functionalist argument that since role specialization is on the increase throughout modern society, "the female sex will not again become more similar to the male" (p. 385). Here, as Jennifer Lehmann notes, Durkheim "qualifies women's 'more active and important' part in society to the point that it becomes meaningless."[40] It is on this issue of limiting divorce that Marx's differences with Durkheim would seem to become the sharpest, given Marx's stress on oppressive family relationships as a major factor in female suicide, and his critique of bourgeois marriage as an oppressive institution that should not be regarded as a fixed universal.

Marx's early article and translation on suicide thus offers a different perspective from that of Durkheim's *Suicide*. Marx suggests that the oppressiveness of the bourgeois family is responsible for many cases of female suicide, especially of young women. Marx's text also helps us to grasp more clearly his emerging views on gender and the family in modern society, during the same period in which he was developing his concepts of alienated labor and historical materialism and the beginnings of his critique of political economy and the state.

Notes

I would like to thank Janet Afary, Dave Black, Franklin Dmitryev, Peter Hudis, Ophra Leyser, Heinz Osterle, Albert Resis, John Rhoads, Jürgen Rojahn, and David Norman Smith for helpful comments, and Marc Rittle for research assistance. Some of the work for this introduction was carried out under an American Council of Learned Societies Fellowship.

1. For background on Peuchet and on Marx's text, I have found especially useful Philippe Bourrinet's introduction and notes to a recent French edition. See Bourrinet, "Présentation," in Marx/Peuchet, *A propos du suicide* (Castelnau-le-Lez: Éditions Climats, 1992), p. 9–27. Another good discussion, the first analysis of this text in any language of which I am aware, is in Jerrold Seigel, *Marx's Fate: The Shape of a Life* (Princeton: Princeton University Press, 1978). Surprisingly, however, neither Bourrinet nor Seigel single out the fact that Marx here concentrates on female suicide.

2. The *Marx-Engels Gesamtausgabe* (hereafter *MEGA*), initiated in the 1920s, ceased to appear after Stalin came to power, and its founding editor, David Riazanov, was imprisoned and later executed. A second *MEGA* was begun with lavish funding from East Berlin and Moscow in 1975, but was still unfinished by the time of Stalinist communism's collapse. Today, it is being continued more slowly, and with new editorial guidelines, under the overall editorship of Western scholars based in Amsterdam. For accounts, see Jacques Grandjonc and Jürgen Rojahn, "Aus der MEGA-Arbeit. Der revidierte Plan der *Marx-Engels Gesamtausgabe*," *MEGA-Studien* 2 (1995), 62–89, and the articles by Rojahn, Rolf Hecker, and Kevin Anderson in *Critique* (Glasgow), nos. 30–31 (1998): 179–207.

3. Karl Marx and Friedrich Engels, *Collected Works* (hereafter *MECW*), vol. 3 (New York: International Publishers, 1975). Although I will usually give in-text references to the Moscow-based *MECW*, which now includes almost fifty volumes, I have sometimes made my own translations or substituted clearer ones from other sources for the wooden or otherwise problematic ones sometimes found in *MECW*. On alienation, see especially István Mészáros, *Marx's Theory of Alienation* (London: Merlin, 1970) and Bertell Ollman, *Alienation* (New York: Cambridge University Press, 1971).

4. In his *History of Marxism*, vol. 1 (New York: Oxford University Press, 1978), Leszek Kolakowski refers repeatedly to Marx's "Promethean . . . faith in man's unlimited powers as self-creator" (p. 412), but as Louis Dupré notes astutely in his *Marx's Social Critique of Culture* (New Haven: Yale University Press, 1983), there is also a hard realism in Marx, "who challenged the pretensions of the modern age, criticizing any view that would detach socialization from its natural basis" (p. 3).

5. Marcuse's 1932 essay appeared in English in his *Studies in Critical Philosophy* (Boston: Beacon Press, 1972). See also Simone de Beauvoir, *The Second Sex* (New York: Alfred A. Knopf, 1952, orig. 1949) and Raya Dunayevskaya, *Rosa Luxemburg, Women's Liberation, and Marx's Philosophy of Revolution*, 2d ed. (Urbana: University of Illinois Press, 1991, orig. 1982). Unfortunately, de Beauvoir construed this passage in such a way as to buttress her own conclusion that men would be the ones to liberate women, writing that "it is for man to establish the reign of liberty" (p. 732). However, such a standpoint cannot be found in Marx's text.

6. I have consistently translated *Mensch* as "human being" rather than "man," to make clear when Marx is discussing human beings as a whole and when he is speaking about the male (*Mann*) or the female (*Weib*). The existing English translations, which were made at a time when "man" was more accepted as a universal term for all human beings than it is today, do not make this distinction consistently. This will allow the reader to see exactly where Marx is speaking of humanity as a whole (*Menschen*), and where he is speaking specifically of man (*Mann*) or woman (*Weib*).

7. Raya Dunayevskaya, *Women's Liberation and the Dialectics of Revolution* (1985; reprint Detroit: Wayne State University Press, 1996, orig. 1985), p. 10.

8. In a letter to Marx of 20 January 1845, Engels acknowledges that he actually wrote less than 10 percent of this book.

9. See the entry on Tristan, who was Paul Gaugin's grandmother, in the *Encyclopedia Universalis* (Paris, 1990).

10. Here Benjamin has cited a 1914 article in *Revue de deux mondes*.

11. Walter Benjamin, *Charles Baudelaire: A Lyric Poet in the Era of High Capitalism*, trans. Harry Zohn (London: New Left Books, 1973), p. 76.

12. Too often, this book and *The German Ideology*, in which Marx and Engels develop stinging critiques of the Young Hegelians, especially Bruno Bauer, Ludwig Feuerbach, and Max Stirner, have been interpreted, wrongly, as a wholesale attack on Hegel as well. However, these books contain many passages pointing to Hegel's standpoint as far superior to that of the Young Hegelians, and they nowhere dismiss Hegel's work, even as they are attacking the idealist form that he gave the dialectic.

13. This passage was written by Engels.

14. G. Bagaturia et al., eds., *MEGA* IV/3 (Berlin: Akademie Verlag, 1998), p. 132.

15. See Hal Draper, "Marx and Engels on Women's Liberation," *International Socialism*, July-August 1970, pp. 20–28. Draper calls attention to this passage, also noting that Engels softened Marx's language on the fam-

ily, changing the word "destroyed" to "criticized," when he published the theses in 1888. (Both versions are now in *MECW* 5.) Unfortunately, Draper passes up many other chances to note important differences between Marx and Engels on gender, too often merging Marx's views with those of Engels or even the utopian socialist Charles Fourier. For critiques of Draper and Engels, see Dunayevskaya, *Women's Liberation.*

16. For a critique of Hess, see Georg Lukács, "Moses Hess and the Problems of Idealist Dialectics," pp. 181–223 in his *Tactics and Ethics: Political Essays, 1919–1929* (New York: Harper and Row, 1975).

17. I base the dating on Hal Draper, who in his usually reliable *Marx-Engels Chronicle* (New York: Schocken, 1985), says that it was written "probably around the last quarter of the year" 1845, and "perhaps as early as September" (pp. 19, 21).

18. Bourrinet, "Présentation," p. 18.

19. See Alexandre Dumas, *Le Comte de Monte-Cristo* (Paris: Éditions Garnier, 1962). This edition's editor, Jacques-Henry Bornecque, includes as an appendix "Le Diamant et la vengeance" (pp. 781–96), the excerpt from Peuchet's *Memoirs* upon which Dumas drew. In Peuchet's supposedly factual account, however, the central character is a shoemaker, not a naval officer.

20. The references in parentheses to "Peuchet on Suicide" are to the present edition.

21. Maximilien Rubel, who includes excerpts from Marx's article and translation on suicide in his edition of Marx's *Oeuvres*, vol. 3 (Paris: Éditions Gallimard, 1982), expresses surprise that Marx does not take up Peuchet's comments, a bit later in his *Memoirs*, on the early communist Gracchus Babeuf, guillotined in 1797. Peuchet, who knew Babeuf personally, wrote that the egoism of the wealthy during the Restoration risked the reappearance not only of the revolution, but also of communist ideas.

22. We have indicated such loose translations and other additions or alterations by Marx in the notes to the text of the translation.

23. It is unclear whether Erich Fromm, Theodor Adorno, Herbert Marcuse, or other members of the Frankfurt School, who in the 1930s developed the concept of the authoritarian personality, had read this passage by Marx. Marx's piece on Peuchet and suicide was included in the 1932 *MEGA* volume, which also contained the *1844 Essays*. Marcuse, who as mentioned above reviewed the *1844 Essays* that year, did not, however, mention the text on Peuchet in his review.

24. See below and the next chapter for more comparison to Durkheim's *Suicide.*

25. For more comprehensive discussions, see especially Dunayevskaya, "Marx's 'New Humanism' and the Dialectics of Women's Liberation in

Primitive and Modern Societies," *Praxis International*, 3(4) (1984): 369–81; Rubel, "L'émancipation des femmes dans l'oeuvre de Marx et d'Engels," in *Encyclopédie politique et historique des femmes*, Christine Fauré, ed. (Paris: Presses Universitaires de France, 1997), pp. 381–403; and Hal Draper, "Marx and Engels on Women's Liberation."

26. Though the standard English translation, carried out in 1888 under Engels's supervision, renders the German word *Aufhebung* here as "abolition," this rather complex German term, often used by Hegel as well, can carry the additional (and in this context slightly softer) meaning of preservation in a higher form. *Aufhebung* has sometimes been rendered as "transcendence," but that creates additional problems. In recent Hegel translations, it has usually been translated as "sublation," an old and somewhat obscure English term that is our closest English equivalent.

27. For background, see Rob Beamish, "The Making of the Manifesto," in *Socialist Register 1998*, ed. Leo Panitch and Colin Leys (New York: Monthly Review Press, 1998), pp. 218–39. Beamish does not view these different texts with regard to the family as indicative of differences between Marx and Engels, however. He stresses instead the degree to which Marx and Engels had not yet attained theoretical leadership within the Communist League by June 1847, and the extent to which Engels "had not been totally successful" (p. 228) in shaping a draft which still included many formulations from a still earlier 1844 "Communist Confession in Questions and Answers" by Moses Hess.

28. Karl Marx, *Capital*, trans. Ben Fowkes, vol. 1 (New York: Vintage, 1976), pp. 620–21.

29. Karl Marx, *The Ethnological Notebooks of Karl Marx*, transcribed and ed. Lawrence Krader (Assen, Netherlands: Van Gorcum, 1974), p. 121. Although I am citing the Krader edition, I am using the full English translation from the Yale University Press version, edited by David Norman Smith, whom I thank for sharing it with me.

30. Here the strong defense of women's equality in book 4 of Plato's *Republic* might be recalled.

31. Marx, *Ethnological Notebooks*, p. 121.

32. Dunayevskaya, *Rosa Luxemburg*, p. 181. See also the discussions of these differences between Marx and Engels on women's liberation, influenced by Dunayevskaya, in Adrienne Rich's foreword to the 1991 edition of Dunayevskaya's *Rosa Luxemburg*, in Rich's *What Is Found There: Notebooks on Poetry and Politics* (New York: Norton, 1993), and in Margaret Randall, *Gathering Rage: The Failure of Twentieth Century Revolutions to Develop a Feminist Agenda* (New York: Monthly Review Press, 1992). See as well, from a somewhat different vantage point, Danga Vilei-

sis, "Engels Rolle im 'unglücklichen Verhältnis' zwischen Marxismus und Feminismus," in *Beiträge zur Marx-Engels-Forschung. Neue Folge 1996* (Berlin: Argument Verlag, 1996), pp. 149–79. Surprisingly, Rubel, often a critic of Engels, opposes any such distinction between Marx and Engels on gender, writing in his "L'émancipation des femmes" that Engels's *Origin of the Family* represents the "final collaboration between the two friends," albeit a "posthumous" one (p. 401). Only a few feminist theorists have taken up the question of differences between Marx and Engels on women's liberation. However, beginning with de Beauvoir's *The Second Sex,* many feminist theorists have attacked Engels's book for its reductionism, in which gender relations are a reflection of property and class forms.

33. The fullest account of these and other general issues related to Durkheim can be found in Steven Lukes, *Émile Durkheim: His Life and Work* (New York: Penguin, 1973).

34. Émile Durkheim, *Suicide: A Study in Sociology,* trans. John Spaulding and George Simpson (1897; trans., New York: Free Press, 1951), p. 209. Further page references directly in the text.

35. For example, at one point in *Capital,* volume 1, Marx criticizes John Stuart Mill, who, he writes, "is as much at home with absurd and flat contradictions as he is at sea with the Hegelian 'contradiction,' which is the source of all dialectic" (p. 744).

36. See Philippe Besnard, "Durkheim et les femmes ou le *Suicide* inachevé," *Revue française de sociologie,* 14:1(1973): 27–61; Terry R. Kandal, *The Woman Question in Classical Sociological Theory* (Miami: Florida International University Press, 1988); Jennifer Lehmann, *Durkheim and Women* (Lincoln: University of Nebraska Press, 1994); and Lehmann, "Durkheim's Theories of Deviance and Suicide: A Feminist Reconsideration," *American Journal of Sociology,* 100(4) (1995): 904–30.

37. Kandal, *The Woman Question,* p. 88.

38. Besnard, "Durkheim et les femmes ou le *Suicide* inachevé," p. 212.

39. Durkheim makes no reference to Peuchet in his *Suicide.*

40. Lehmann, "Durkheim's Theories of Deviance and Suicide," pp. 919–20.

Marx on Suicide in the Context of Other Views of Suicide and of His Life

Eric A. Plaut

I wish to address Karl Marx's view of suicide from three perspectives: its relationship to the literature on suicide, the issue of suicide in the Marx family, and the connection between these two and Marx's worldview.

Studies of suicide usually approach the topic from either a psychological or a sociological perspective. Freud is the éminence grise of the psychological perspective, Durkheim of the sociological. The literature on suicide is immense,[1] and no review of it can be attempted here. And, sad to say, none would be very illuminating. For the twentieth century, although it has brought many modifications and elaborations of Freud's and Durkheim's views, has not produced either insight or methodology that has greatly increased our understanding of suicide beyond that contained in their work. Accordingly, I shall confine my discussion to locating Marx's view in relationship to their views.

Paradoxically, neither Durkheim nor Freud was particularly interested in suicide. Durkheim wrote his seminal book, entitled *Suicide*,[2] not primarily as a contribution to the literature on the topic, but rather because suicide was a convenient example for illustrating his methodology of sociology. He subtitled the work *A Study in Sociology*.

Similarly, in the index to the twenty-three volumes of Freud's collected works there are only five citations to suicide itself.[3] There are many more to suicidal ideation, because it was not the act of suicide that primarily interested Freud but the psychic activity that lies underneath.

In Marx's oeuvre, the essay is somewhat unusual in two ways. What most commonly stimulated him to write was disagreement with someone. He wrote angry polemics against Bauer, Weitling, Stirner, Proudhon, Grün, Hess, Bakunin, Vogt, and Lassalle. In contrast, his view of Peuchet is clearly favorable. Also, the bulk of the essay is a translation from the French. Even for such a superb linguist as Marx, translation is a tedious task, particularly for a perfectionist like Marx. Two reasons are usually cited for his decision to undertake this project: He clearly shared Peuchet's view of the destructive nature of the existing society, and he intended the essay as a criticism of German social theorists. In addition to these conscious motivations, I believe Marx had an unconscious concern with suicide, a topic I shall return to below.

Although Freud discussed many aspects of suicide and suicide ideation,[4] he always returned to his basic conceptualization: "Probably no one finds the mental energy to kill himself unless, in the first place, in doing so he is at the same time killing an object with whom he has identified himself and, in the second place, is turning against himself a death wish which had been directed against someone else."[5] In Litman's words, "There are, according to Freud, general features of the human condition, at least in Western civilization, which make each individual person somewhat vulnerable to suicide."[6] This vulnerability exists because aggression against the self is an integral aspect of human development. It ranges from the totally normal to the seriously pathological; from a healthy conscience to overconscientiousness, to moral masochism, to depressive and suicidal ideation, to suicide itself.

For Freud the understanding of suicide could come only from the understanding of intrapsychic processes. It was an issue for psychology. He had little respect for sociology, calling it "applied psychology."[7] At the same time, the influence of society on the development of the human psyche was integral to his thinking. He devoted his *Civilization and Its Discontents* to the topic.[8] And in his "Contribution to a Discussion on Suicide"[9] he explicitly included the maladministration of a school as an etiologic factor in the suicide of an adolescent.

For Durkheim, since the incidence of suicide varied so widely in different places, the suicide rate could not be understood psychologically, only sociologically. Like Freud, he considered many factors to be involved. Maris identified eighteen different factors mentioned by Durkheim.[10] Although he mentioned some exceptions, Durkheim focused on three types of suicide: the altruistic, the egoistical, and the anomic. The altruistic form was seen as rare in Western civilization. The distinction between the egoistical and the anomic is far from clear in his work[11] and disappears in his one summary statement of his view: "Suicide varies inversely with the degree of integration of the social groups of which the individual forms a part."[12]

In Durkheim's usage, the term "anomie" refers to the lack of integration of those social groups. Unlike other authors,[13] he regards it as a purely sociologic concept; it is a characteristic of societies, not of individuals. Anomie as a cause of suicide was illustrative of a general principle stated in one of his earlier works: "The determining cause of a social fact should be sought among the social facts preceding it, and not among the states of the individual consciousness."[14]

Durkheim was not as dismissive of psychology as Freud was of sociology, but he was not willing to attribute any causative role in suicide to psychological forces. The closest he came was in his identification of a "collective inclination to suicide."[15] He also called it a "collective disposition" which exists "normally in every society."[16] His concept of a normally existing disposition to suicide has considerable resonance with Freud's concept of aggression against the self as a normal phenomenon. Similarly, they both saw a loosening of ties to the outside world as a causative factor. For Freud it was the abandonment of emotional investment in an outside object in favor of investment in an internalized object; for Durkheim it was the loosening of ties to society because of society's anomic state. Finally, both shared a view of the relative impotence of human consciousness vis-à-vis the unconscious. It was central to all of Freud's thinking. He could well have written Durkheim's words on the topic: "Human deliberations, in fact, so far as reflective consciousness affects them are often purely formal, with no object but confirmation of a resolve previously formed for reasons unknown to consciousness."[17] Marx had the same insight half a century earlier. Berlin summarized Marx's view: "In the attempt to convince themselves that their acts are determined by reason or by moral or religious beliefs, men have tended to construct elaborate rationalizations of their behavior."[18]

In both content and form, Marx's essay stands halfway between Freud and Durkheim. Although he does not use the term "alienation" in the essay, Marx clearly views it as the cause of the suicides—for example, the husband who treats his wife as "inventory" (see "Peuchet on Suicide," p. 58) and the man who commits suicide because he has lost his job (see p. 67). It is beyond the scope of these comments to address the complex issue of how narrowly or how broadly Marx defined alienation. On the one hand, he seemed to limit it to the lot of the worker under capitalism, as in his critique in the *Communist Manifesto*, of those who defined it more broadly. On the other hand, many

Marx scholars see it as lying at the heart of his worldview.[19] In this essay, Marx explicitly embraces the broader view in that he specifically includes the bourgeoisie among those suffering under the existing social conditions (see p. 45). In that they both view the evils of existing society as the causative factor in suicide, Durkheim's perspective is the same as Marx's.

There are, however, three important differences between Durkheim's and Marx's concepts. Anomie is a characteristic of societies, not of individuals. Hence it is a social fact. Alienation is a characteristic of individuals, albeit caused by society. Hence it is a psychological, not a social, fact. In the second place, in anomie man is disconnected from society, whereas in alienation he is too connected to society and thereby alienated from his true self. In his *Civilization and Its Discontents* Freud embraces both perspectives. As already mentioned, man has abandoned the real (social) object for an internal one. However, his discontent is also because he is alienated from his true self, the expression of his instincts. Finally, for Marx, the existing society causes suicide, whereas for Durkheim, it fails to prevent it. Or, to put it another way, for Marx the issue was the presence of social conflict; for Durkheim it was the absence of social cohesion.

The form of the essay also places Marx halfway between Durkheim and Freud. Although he strongly supports almost all of Peuchet's views of society and all the alterations Marx makes of Peuchet's original are in discussions of society, the bulk of the essay is devoted to case vignettes consisting primarily of detailed examinations of the complexities of human motivation. Such vignettes are typical of Freud's work and highly atypical of Durkheim's, and they appear only occasionally in Marx. It seems likely that Marx went to the trouble of translating them, rather than just discussing Peuchet's social views, because they touched him personally, albeit probably unconsciously.

There is no evidence that Marx was ever consciously suicidal himself, but there is a great deal of evidence that suicide was very much an issue in the Marx family. As early as during Marx's long engagement to Jenny von Westphalen, Marx's father saw in her "a fear, a presentiment . . . that worried him."[20] In a letter to Engels, Marx wrote, "My wife tells me every day that she wishes she and the children were in their graves."[21] Although his wife did not commit suicide, two of his three adult daughters, Laura and Eleanor, did, late in their lives. (The other daughter, Jenny, died of cancer in 1883, the same year as her father. Whether or not she was suicidal is unclear.)[22] Eleanor had a long history of depression and at least one known suicide attempt before her successful suicide. Laura and her husband died in a suicide pact.

Throughout much of the world, folk wisdom has considered suicide a form of murder. In the Romance languages the word is derived from the Latin *sui* (self) and *caedere* (kill). In German it is the same: *selbstmord* (self-murder). In Japanese the word is *jisatsu*, the two characters for "self " and "kill." In Freud's view, the suicidal impulse always reflects an earlier murderous one. Such primitive, unmodified aggression may, in any given individual, be primarily directed inward or outward. Inevitably, both forms are present, although frequently one is expressed overtly, the other covertly. The same is true of less primitive forms of aggression.

Karl Marx was neither murderous nor suicidal. He was, however, an extremely angry man. Engels once described him as a "remarkable monster" who "blusters full of rage."[23] Retrospective psychobiography is always a risky undertaking, particularly regarding someone like Marx, about whose early years so little is known. No attempt will be made here to speculate on the childhood origins of Marx's rage. There is, however, abundant information both about the overt outward direction of that rage and about its covert inward direction in Marx as an adult. Seigel describes that duality this way: "Struggle and submission, egoism and self-sacrifice were the organizing poles of his experience."[24] McLellan, discussing Marx's year-long battle with Karl Vogt, called it "a striking example both of Marx's ability to expend tremendous labor on essentially trivial matters and also his talent for vituperation."[25]

As already noted, Marx did much of his writing in the form of angry polemics against others. Not surprisingly, he was rarely able to sustain friendly relations with colleagues, the most important exception being the ever-faithful Engels. His anger also showed itself in his choice of words. It was not enough that things needed to be changed. They had to be "destroyed," "annihilated," "abolished," "burst asunder." He closed his *Poverty of Philosophy* with a quote from George Sand: "Combat or death; bloody battle or nothing."[26] Marx's open aggression was noted so extensively in his lifetime, as well as posthumously by his biographers, that it needs no further discussion here.

Far less attention has been paid to his self-destructiveness, although it has been discussed by a number of writers. Manuel's term was "self-loathing,"[27] Seigel's was "self-sacrifice,"[28] and Künzli's was "self-hate."[29] Freud's term for (nonsexualized) aggression against the self was "moral masochism." The moral masochist is one who "must act against his own interests, must ruin the prospects which open out to him in the real world and must, perhaps, destroy his own real existence."[30] Marx never destroyed his existence, but he certainly acted against his own interests and ruined many of his prospects.

Marx's masochism manifested itself in numerous areas— finances, health, marriage, and work. He never established a reliable way of supporting himself and his family. The income from his writing was intermittent. The family lived beyond its means and was frequently on the edge of bank-ruptcy, forestalled only by money from Engels. Marx's neglect of his health had already been an issue of concern to his parents when he was a young man. In later life he was subjected to repeated episodes of carbuncles. Instructions from his doctors to lead an orderly life, eat a normal diet, not stay up all night, and take his medications regularly were never heeded for long. Marx was aware of the role his emotions played in his health problems. He wrote to Engels from a spa where he had sought treatment "the real trouble is of a psychic nature."[31]

Although he clearly was a devoted father to his daughters, Marx frequently complained bitterly about his family life. Much of the conflict was undoubtedly due to the frequent financial crises. As always, it is difficult to assess the quality of a marriage from afar. However, the fact that Marx fathered a son by the family's longtime housekeeper suggests that the problems were more than financial. Although the boy later became friendly with his half-sister, Eleanor, Marx never concerned himself with him.

Of greatest importance to the world is the extent to which Marx's masochism interfered with his work. He frequently had great difficulty completing a project. Although physical health problems undoubtedly played a role, Marx attributed the problem to his "peculiarity that if I look at something I finished writing four weeks afterward, I find it insufficient and do the work all over again."[32] Engels repeatedly implored him to stop revising and send his manuscripts off to the publishers. It took Marx many years to complete volume 1 of *Das Kapital.* During these years the work often lay almost untouched. Indeed, had it not been for Engels's importunings and for the ultimately unrealized hope for substantial royalties, Marx might never have completed it. He never did finish volumes 2 and 3.

Although Marx viewed women generally as an oppressed group, he may also have felt a specific personal identification with the suicidal women in Peuchet's vignettes. His daughter Eleanor (Tussy) was the most overtly suicidal member of the family. Marx is reported as having said, "Jenny is most like me, but Tussy . . . is me."[33] Additionally, although Marx always wrote from the perspective of the proletariat, he was raised and lived all his life, insofar as finances permitted, as a member of the bourgeoisie. Whatever guilt he felt about the emotional problems of the women in his family may also have inclined him to identify with the bourgeois males who are the villains in the vignettes. Since Marx altered Peuchet's essay in so many places, his presenting it as a straight translation of Peuchet was somewhat disingenuous. If, as I am suggesting, Marx had strong and very painful feelings about suicide, presenting the essay as Peuchet's words rather than his own may have allowed him to express his feelings without fully acknowledging ownership of them.

Marx's worldview was apocalyptic.[34] The coming revolution was not to be just another one in the long history of class struggle; it was to be the ultimate revolution. The proletariat was the final class. The institutions of family and state would be destroyed. The inherent contradictions in capitalist society made its collapse inevitable. In the 1840s he was convinced that the final revolution was at hand. In his view, the capitalist system had evolved to the point where its demise was imminent. When the revolutions of 1848 and the many subsequent upheavals in the second half of the nineteenth century failed to bring the final revolution about, Marx changed his view of the timing. The realities of his era, as well as his more sophisticated understanding of capitalism, led him to realize that the existing system was more resilient than he had originally thought, and so the timing of its dissolution could not be predicted. But his inner need to retain the apocalyptic vision was too great to allow him to abandon it.

In the traditional religious version of the Apocalypse, it is followed by the ascent to heaven of the deserving. In Marx's version, it is followed by the ideal society of communism. Marx was a brilliant critic of existing society. On the subject of how communism would actually function, he had little to say. His psychological makeup was not adapted to that task. Deconstruction, not construction, was his forte. He never spelled out in any detail how the proletarian revolution would evolve into true communism. To date, that has not happened. Instead, it has been capitalism, with all its faults, that has flourished. It has retained the resiliency that Marx came to understand but which he could not fully accept.

From Durkheim's perspective, Marx would have been someone vulnerable to suicide. He lived in a turbulent era. He moved from Germany to France to Belgium to England. He went from Judaism to Christianity to atheism. He alienated most of his colleagues. His attempts to form a stable group of adherents did not succeed. His family relationships were fraught with conflict. His lifeworld was certainly anomic.

From Freud's perspective, Marx's emotional life was pervaded by aggression. Its outward expression was reflected in his behavior and his writings. Its inward expression, although never manifested by actually suicidal behavior, took its toll in his lifelong, self-defeating tendencies. In *Das Kapital* Marx was able to put his rage at the service of his genius and create a masterpiece that retains its relevance to this day. His little essay on suicide contains much that can cast light not only on its topic, but also on its remarkable author and his important work.

Notes

1. For a well organized bibliography of the literature see John L. McIntosh, *Suicide: A Bibliography* (Westport, Conn.: Greenwood Press, 1985). For an overview of psychological perspectives see John T. Maltsberger and Mark J. Goldblatt, *Essential Papers on Suicide* (New York: New York University Press, 1996). For an overview and critique of the sociological literature see J. Maxwell Atkinson, *Discovering Suicide* (Pittsburgh: University of Pittsburgh Press, 1978).

2. Émile Durkheim, *Suicide: A Study in Sociology*, trans. John Spaulding and George Simpson (1897; trans., New York, Free Press, 1951).

3. Sigmund Freud, *The Standard Edition of the Complete Psychological Works of Sigmund Freud* (hereafter *SE*), trans. James Strachey, vol. 24 (London: Hogarth Press,1974).

4. For a good summary of Freud's views see Robert E. Litman, "Freud on Suicide," in Maltsberger and Goldblatt, *Essential Papers on Suicide*, pp. 200–20.

5. *SE*, vol. 18, 162.

6. Litman, "Freud on Suicide," p. 214.

7. *SE*, vol. 18, p. 71.

8. Ibid., vol. 21, pp. 64–148.

9. Ibid., vol. 11, pp. 231–32.

10. Ronald Maris, *Social Forces in Urban Suicide* (Homewood, Ill.: Dorsey Press, 1969), pp. 32–33.

11. See, for example, A. R. Manson, "Durkheim and Contemporary Pathology," *British Journal of Sociology* 21 (1970): 298–313, who subsumes both the egotistical and the anomic under the concept "normlessness" and Shlomo Avineri, *The Social and Political Thought of Karl Marx* (London: Cambridge University Press, 1970), who subsumes them under the concept "state of disaggregation."

12. Durkheim, *Suicide*, p. 209.

13. See particularly Robert K. Merton, *Social Theory and Social Structure* (Glencoe, Ill.: Free Press, 1957). For a critique of both Durkheim and Merton see Donald L. Levine, *The Flight from Ambiguity* (Chicago: University of Chicago Press, 1985).

14. Émile Durkheim, *The Rules of Sociological Method* (Glencoe, Ill.: Free Press, 1938), p. 110.

15. Durkheim, *Suicide*, p. 302.

16. Ibid., p. 132.

17. Ibid., p. 297.

18. Isaiah Berlin, *Karl Marx* (New York: Time Inc., 1963), p. 113.

19. Berlin, *Karl Marx*; Raya Dunayevskaya, *Marxism and Freedom* (New York: Columbia University Press, 1988); Erich Fromm, *Marx's Concept of Man* (New York: Continuum, 1991).

20. Cited in Jerrold Seigel, *Marx's Fate* (Princeton: Princeton University Press, 1978), p.55.

21. Marx to Engels, 20 January 1864, *Marx-Engels Gesamtausgabe*, vol. 3 (1930), p. 164.

22. For references to Jenny's emotional makeup, see Seigel, *Marx's Fate*, p. 429, n.64.

23. Gustav Mayer, *Friedrich Engels: Eine Biographie*, 2d ed. (Cologne, Germany: Kiepenheur und Witsch, 1971), 1:85.

24. Seigel, *Marx's Fate*, p. 376.

25. David McLellan, *Karl Marx, His Life and Thought* (London and New York: Harper & Row, 1973), pp. 311ff.

26. Karl Marx, *The Poverty of Philosophy* (New York: International University Press, 1963), p. 175.

27. Frank E. Manuel, *A Requiem for Karl Marx* (Cambridge, Mass.: Harvard University Press, 1995).

28. Seigel, *Marx's Fate*.

29. Arnold Künzli, *Karl Marx: Eine Psychographie* (Vienna: Europa Verlag, 1966).

30. *SE*, vol. 19, pp. 169–70.

31. Marx to Engels, 17 August 1877, *Marx-Engels-Werke*, vol. 34 (Berlin: Dietz Verlag, 1966), p. 71.

32. Ibid., vol. 30, p. 622.

33. Chushici Tsuzuki, *The Life of Eleanor Marx* (New York: Oxford University Press, 1967), p. 63.

34. For a different perspective on Marx and the apocalyptic worldview, see Ernst Bloch, *Man on His Own*, (New York: Herder and Herder, 1970).

II MARX ON SUICIDE

Peuchet on Suicide

Karl Marx

English translation by
Eric A. Plaut, Gabrielle Edgcomb, and Kevin Anderson

A Note on the English Translation

In this translation, wherever Marx added to Peuchet's original, the additions and major substitutions are in bold type. Italics conform to Marx's emphasis in the original.

Wherever Marx omitted material from Peuchet, we have included a translation of the missing French text in a footnote. The footnote symbol appears within the text at the point at which the omission occurs. For example, if Marx omitted Peuchet's words at the beginning of a paragraph, the footnote symbol precedes that paragraph. We employ the standard footnote symbols: asterisk (*), dagger (†), double dagger (‡), section symbol (§), parallels (‖), and pound sign (#).

Our explanatory comments are identified by numerals and can be found in the note section at the end of this selection (see p. 71). On the question of whether to opt for the best current English usage, at the risk of being less literal, or the opposite, we have leaned toward remaining as close to the original as possible, at the cost of sometimes less than ideal current English. However, in keeping with standard practice in translations from German, we have broken up some of the longer German paragraphs.

Marx's essay has had a somewhat unusual history. First published in Gesellschaftsspiegel *in 1846, it was not reprinted during his lifetime. It is not even mentioned in any of the surviving letters between him and his colleagues during the period when it was published. It was reprinted in German in Moscow in 1932, with very minimal scholarly notes, in volume I/3 of the* Marx-Engels Gesamtausgabe (MEGA). *This volume included, more notably, the "Economic and Philosophical Manuscripts" and "The Holy Family."*

Surprisingly, the text on Peuchet and suicide was not included at all in the East German Marx-Engels Werke *(1956–68), a somewhat less complete edition than what had been projected for the* MEGA. *The latter edition had ceased publication during the 1930s. The first English translation appeared in 1975 in volume 4 of the Moscow-based* Marx and Engels Collected Works, *but once again, with few scholarly notes. The second* MEGA, *begun in East Berlin and Moscow in 1975 and continuing today under Western editorship and with new editorial guidelines, has not yet published the volume which will include this text. Maximilien Rubel published an abbreviated French edition in 1983 in volume 3 of his* Marx Oeuvres, *in which he also included four pages of explanatory notes. In 1992, Marx/Peuchet,* A propos du suicide, *appeared in French. This small book included editor Philippe Bourrinet's introduction, editorial notes, and other background material such as the 1838 preface to Peuchet's* Memoires. *Peuchet's* Memoires tirés des archives de la police *(1838) has never been reprinted. For the present edition, we have relied mainly upon Marx's original 1846 publication as well as Peuchet's 1838 text, but we have consulted all of the later editions.*

The first draft of this translation was jointly done by Eric Plaut and Gabrielle Edgcomb. Unfortunately, Ms. Edgcomb died early in 1997. The final translation and any errors therein are thus the sole responsibility of the editors. Additional assistance with the translation was provided by the late Donald McIntosh, Lily Fahoud, Monique LeMaitre, Claire Lindenlaub, and Philip Hersh.

Eric A. Plaut and Kevin Anderson

French critique of society has, at least partly, the great advantage of demonstrating the contradictions and the unnatural state of modern life, not only in the relationship between particular classes, but also in all spheres and forms of current intercourse.[1] Indeed, their descriptions have a direct warmth of feeling, a richness of intuition, a worldly sensitivity and insightful originality for which one searches in vain in all other nations. One need only compare, for example, the critical descriptions of Owen[2] and Fourier,[3] insofar as they deal with actual intercourse to get a picture of the superiority of the French. It is by no means only the "socialist" French writers among whom one should look for these critical descriptions of social conditions. Included are writers of every type of literature, particularly those of fiction and biography. I shall use an excerpt about *suicide* from the *Memoirs* drawn from the *Police Archives* by Jacques Peuchet as an example of French critique. At the same time, it may show the extent to which it is the conceit of the benevolent bourgeoisie that the only issues are providing some bread and some education to the proletariat, as if only the workers suffer from present social conditions, but that, in general, this is the best of all possible worlds.

With Jacques Peuchet, as with many older French practitioners (now mostly deceased) who lived through the numerous upheavals since 1789—the numerous deceptions, enthusiasms, constitutions, rulers, defeats, and victories—there appeared a critique of the existing property, family, and other private relationships (in a word, of private life) as the necessary consequence of their political experiences.

Jacques Peuchet (born 1760) went from the fine arts to medicine, from medicine to law, from law to administration and police work.

Before the outbreak of the French revolution he worked, with the Abbé Morellet,[4] on a *Dictionnaire du Commerce*

of which only a prospectus appeared, and he preferred deal-
ing with political economy and administration. He was a
supporter of the French Revolution but only briefly. He
soon turned to the royalist party, was for a time the direc-
tor of the *Gazette de France*[5] and later even took over, from
Mallet-du-Pan,[6] the infamous, royalist *Mercure.*[7] Cleverly
wending his way through the French Revolution, sometimes persecuted, then occupied in the Department of
Administration and the Police, his five-volume *Géographie
commerçante* (published in 1800) drew the attention of
Bonaparte, the First Consul, and he was appointed a member of the *Council of Commerce and the Arts.* Later, during
the ministry of François von Neufchâteau,[8] he assumed a
higher administrative position. In 1814 the Restoration
appointed him censor. During the 100 days[9] he withdrew.
With the reinstatement of the Bourbons, he attained the
position of archivist of the Paris Prefecture of Police, a position he held until 1827.[10] Peuchet was directly involved,
and, as a writer, not without influence on the spokesmen
for the Constituent Assembly,[11] the Convention, the Tri-
bunate, and, under the Restoration, the Chamber of
Deputies. Among his many, mostly economic works, in
addition to the aforementioned commercial-geography, his
Statistique de la France (1807)[12] is best known.

As an *old man,* Peuchet drafted his memoirs, partly from
materials from the Paris Police Archives, partly from his
long practical experience in police work and administration, but insisted they be published *only posthumously.*
Thus, under no circumstances can he be included among
those *"premature"* socialists and communists who, as is
well known, lack so totally the wonderful thoroughness
and the all-encompassing knowledge of the vast majority of
our writers, officials, and practical citizens.

Listen then to our archivist of the Paris Police Prefecture
on the subject of *suicide:*

The yearly toll of suicides, which is to some extent normal and periodic, has to be viewed as a symptom of the deficient organization* of our society. For, in times of industrial stagnation and its crises, in times of high food prices and hard winters, this symptom always becomes more prominent and takes on an epidemic character. At these times, prostitution and theft increase proportionately. Although penury is the greatest source of suicide, we find it in all classes, among the idle rich, as well as among artists and politicians. The varieties of reasons motivating suicide make a mockery of the moralists' single-minded and uncharitable blaming.

Consumptive illnesses, against which present-day science is inadequate and ineffective, abused friendship, betrayed love, discouraged ambition, family troubles, repressed rivalry, the surfeit of a monotonous life, enthusiasm turned against itself. These are all surely causes of suicide for natures of greater breadth. The love of life itself, the energetic force of personality, often leads to releasing oneself from a contemptible existence.

Madame de Stael,[13] whose greatest service was to beautifully stylize commonplace fictions, was eager to demonstrate that suicide is contrary to nature and that it cannot be understood as an act of courage. Above all, she argued that it is more worthy to fight despair than to give in to it. Such reasoning has little effect upon those souls who are overwhelmed by misfortune. If they are religious, they may be thinking about a better world: if they believe in nothing they may be seeking the peace of nothingness. Philosophical tirades have little value in their eyes and are a poor refuge from suffering. Above all, it is absurd to claim that an act, which occurs so often, is an unnatural act. Suicide is in no way unnatural, as we witness it daily. What is con-

* In Peuchet: "fundamental defect."

trary to nature does not occur. It lies, on the contrary, *in the nature of our society* to cause so many suicides, while* the Tartars do not commit suicide. *Not all societies bring forth the same results.* We must keep this in mind in working to reform our society to allow it to reach a higher level.† What characterizes courage, when one, designated as courageous, confronts death in the light of day on the battlefield, under the sway of mass excitement, is not necessarily lost, when one kills oneself in dark solitude. One does not resolve such a difficult issue by insulting the dead.‡

All that has been said against suicide stems from the same circle of ideas.§ **One condemns suicide with foregone conclusions. But, the very existence of suicide is an open protest against these unsophisticated conclusions.** They speak of our duty to this society, but not of our right to expect explanations and actions by our society. They endlessly exalt, as the infinitely higher virtue, overcoming suffering, rather than giving in to it. Such a virtue is every bit as sad as the perspective it opens up. In brief, one has made suicide an act of cowardice, a crime against law, **society**, and honor.

---

* the Berbers and

† In the destiny of humankind

‡ Whether the motive for the individual suicide is weak or otherwise, one cannot measure sensitivity on the same scale for all men. Evidently one cannot conclude that all feelings, personalities, or temperaments are the same. An event unlikely to disturb some people could trigger a violent reaction in others. Happiness or unhappiness comes in as many different forms as there are people or minds. A poet once said:

> What pleases you would soon torment me;
> The price of your virtue would punish me.

§ One opposes Divine Providence to suicide, without really forcing us to understand its decrees clearly, since after all, those who commit suicide must doubt them. Those who did not clarify this Providence and make it satisfying to others may very well be guilty. The Gospel diamond still remains in its clay.

How is it that people commit suicide, despite such great anathema against it? The blood of the despairing does not flow through the same arteries as that of those cold beings who have the leisure to debate such fruitless questions.*
Man is a mystery to man; one knows only how to blame him, but one does not know him.† Has one noticed how mindless the institutions are under whose rule Europe lives? How they dispose of the life and blood of the people? How civilized justice surrounds itself with large numbers of prisons, physical punishments, and instruments of death to enforce its doubtful arrests? How one observes the shocking number of classes left in misery by all concerned? How social pariahs are dealt brutal, preventive, contemptuous blows, perhaps so one does not have to take the trouble to pull them out of their dirt? When one has noted all these things, one cannot comprehend how, in the name of what authority, an individual can be ordered to care about an existence that our customs, our prejudices, our laws, and our mores trample under foot.

‡ It has been believed that suicide could be prevented by abusive punishments and by branding with infamy the memory of the guilty one. What can one say about the indignity of such branding, hurled at people who are no longer there to plead their case? The unfortunate rarely

---

*It may be that all causes of suicide have not yet been studied. There has not been enough examination of the subversions of the soul in these terrible moments and especially how deadly long periods of suffering can be for a person.

†In Peuchet: "ignore," not *ne connait.*

‡Whatever the determining motive of suicide may be, it is certain that its action has an absolute power over the will. So why be astonished if until now everything that has been said or done to conquer this blind drive has remained powerless and if our legislators' and moralists' attempts have also failed. The understanding of the human heart can only be achieved if one possesses the quality of mercy and the compassion of Jesus.

bother themselves with all this. And, if the act of suicide accuses someone,* it is usually those remaining behind, because in this crowd there was not one person for whom it was worth staying alive. Have the childish and cruel means, that have been devised, successfully fought against the whisperings of despair? To one who wishes to flee this world, how do the insults that the world promises to heap on his corpse matter? *He sees therein only another act of cowardice on the part of the living. In fact, what kind of society is it wherein one finds the most profound loneliness in the midst of many millions of people, a society where one can be overwhelmed by an uncontrollable urge to kill oneself without anyone of us suspecting it! This society is no society, but, as Rousseau† said, a desert populated by wild animals.* In the positions in police administration that I have held,‡ suicides were part of my responsibilities. I wanted to find out if, among the determining causes, one might find some whose consequences could prove to be§ prevented. I undertook a comprehensive study of this subject. **I found that, short of a total reform of the organization of our current society, all other attempts would be in vain.**‖ Among the sources for the despair that leads easily excitable people, passionate beings with deep feelings, to seek death, I found the primary cause was the bad treatment, the injustices, the secret punishments that these people received at the hands of harsh parents and superiors,# upon whom they were dependent. *The revolution did not*

---

* before God (in Peuchet: "vis-à-vis")

† Peuchet writes "Jean-Jacques," but Marx writes "Rousseau."

‡ Following up

§ moderated or

‖ Marx here substitutes his own sentence for Peuchet's, which read: "Without dwelling on theories, I will try to present facts."

In Peuchet: "harsh and biased parents, angry and threatening superiors."

topple all tyrannies. The evil which one blames on arbitrary forces exists in families, where it causes crises, analogous to those of revolutions.

*We must first create, *from the ground up*, the connections between the interests and dispositions, the true relations among individuals. *Suicide is only one of the thousand and one symptoms of the general social struggle ever fought out on new ground.* Many warriors withdraw from this battle, because they are tired of being counted among the victims or† to take a place of honor among the hangmen. If you want some examples, I will draw them from authentic police proceedings.

In the month of July 1816 the daughter of a tailor became engaged to a butcher. He was a young man of good morals, frugal and hardworking. He was very taken with his beau-

---

* Can one be sure, as it is commonly believed, that the fear of seeing one's friends, parents, or servants subjected to infamy, and their bodies dragged through the mud, could bring these pitiless men to be more prudent, moderate, and fair toward their subordinates, and to go so far as to prevent these voluntary murders, committed in order to extract oneself from their domination? I do not think so. Believing this would only be a double blasphemy, and would refuse due respect to both the living and the dead. It is hard to see how such a method could succeed; wisely, it has been renounced.

In order to improve the attitude of superiors toward their subordinates, especially that of the parents among the former, it has been thought that the fear of seeing oneself hit by aspersion and public scandal would be an effective measure. This measure would not suffice. The bitter blame that one gladly pours over the unfortunate one, who has taken his life, diminishes among those who instigated the suicide. However, it does not extinguish this feeling in them, the shame brought by all the scandals, and the awareness of having been the true instigators of the suicide. It seems to me that the clergy is even less religious than society, when it sides with these cowardly prejudices by refusing a religious burial.

In sum,

† Marx here substitutes "or" for Peuchet's "and."

tiful fiancée. She in turn was much drawn to him. She was a seamstress and was held in high esteem by all who knew her, and the parents of her bridegroom loved her dearly. These good people missed no opportunity to anticipate the arrival of their daughter-in-law. They threw many parties wherein she was queen and idol.[*]

The time for the wedding approached. All arrangements between the families had been completed and the contracts signed. The night before the day set for the trip to city hall, the young daughter and her parents were to have dinner with the bridegroom's family. An unimportant event unexpectedly interfered. The tailor and his wife had to stay home—customers from a rich house had to be taken care of. They excused themselves; but the butcher's mother[†] came herself to pick up her daughter-in-law, who had received permission to follow her.

Despite the absence of two of the guests of honor, the dinner turned out to be one of the jolliest. The anticipation of the wedding occasioned the telling of many family anecdotes.[‡] People drank; people sang. The future was discussed. **The joys of a good marriage were the subject of lively discussion.** Very late at night, all were still around the dining table. The parents of the young people, in an easily understandable indulgence,[§] closed their eyes to the still secret[‖] understanding of the engaged couple. Hands sought each other.[#] Love and intimacy were on their minds.

---

[*] Public esteem reinforced the esteem that both of the betrothed bore for each other.

[†] Insisted and

[‡] The mother-in-law was already viewing herself as the godmother of a plump boy.

[§] and overjoyed by their mutual endearments

[‖] In Peuchet: "tacit"

[#] It started like a brush fire.

Besides, the marriage was a foregone conclusion and these young people had been visiting each other for a long time, without giving the slightest reason for reproach.* The sympathy of the lovers' parents, the advanced hour, the mutual longing (set free by the compassion of their mentors), the unabashed joyousness that reigns at such repasts, the wine spinning around in their heads, the opportunity that smilingly beckoned, all these combined to end in an easily anticipated result. After the lights were dimmed, the lovers found themselves in the dark. One pretended to notice nothing; they had no inkling. Here their happiness had only friends, no envious witnesses.†

It was the next morning before the daughter returned to her parents. That she returned alone is evidence that she had no sense of wrongdoing.‡ She slipped into her room and performed her ablutions. No sooner had her parents noticed her, than they furiously poured scandalous names and cursewords on her. The neighborhood witnessed all this: there were no limits to the scandal. The child was shattered by these judgments; her modesty and her privacy were outrageously assaulted. The dismayed girl pointed out to her parents that they themselves brought blame upon her, that she admitted her wrong, her foolishness, her disobedience, but that all would be set to rights. Her reasons and her pain did not disarm their fury. **Those who are most cowardly, who are least capable of resistance themselves, become unyielding as soon as they *can exert absolute parental authority.***

* Never had the pleasures of a good marriage been analyzed so vividly.

† Meaning became more important than form, and this half-stolen pleasure must only have been sweeter.

‡ Her offense was great, no doubt. If only she had considered her relatives' concern about the long absence; but if only kindness, indulgence, prudence, and restraint were forced upon parents for a child, this would have been the case, considering the fact that all circumstances were about to legitimize the amorous escapade. Guiltier ones have been happier.

The abuse of *that authority* also serves as a *cruel substitute* for all the submissiveness and dependency people in bourgeois society acquiesce in, willingly or unwillingly. Neighborhood men and women, drawn to the uproar, supplied a chorus. This awful scene aroused such feelings of shame, that the child decided to take her own life. In the midst of the **crowd's** cursing and scolding, she rushed down to the Seine and, with a crazed look in her eyes, threw herself into the river. The boat people pulled out her dead body still adorned with wedding jewelry. Not surprisingly, those who had been screaming at the daughter, now turned against the parents. The catastrophe scared these **empty** souls. A few days later the parents came to the Police Bureau's depository to reclaim that which had clearly belonged to their child—a gold necklace that had been a present from her future father-in-law, as well as a silver watch, earrings, and a ring with a small emerald, all objects deposited with the police, as would have been expected. I did not fail forcefully to throw up to them their foolishness and barbarity. Telling these infuriated ones that they would be accountable to God would have made little impression, given their hard-hearted prejudices and their particular **kind*** of religiosity, so common among the lower mercantile classes.

It was greed that drew them to my office, not the claim to ownership of a few relics. And, it was through their greed that I thought I could punish them. They claimed their daughter's jewelry; I refused to give it to them. In order to get the jewelry which, according to the regulations, had been placed in the depository they needed a certificate that was in my possession. So long as I held my position their claims were in vain. I enjoyed defying their attacks on me.†

---

* Here Marx radically changes the meaning by replacing "kind" for Peuchet's "lack."

† It was only after my retirement that they were able to obtain remittance.

That same year there appeared in my office a very attrac-
tive young Creole from one of Martinique's richest families.* He was absolutely opposed to our releasing the corpse
of a young woman, his sister-in-law, to its claimant, the
lady's husband and his own brother. She had drowned herself. This is the most common form of suicide. The officers
assigned to fishing the corpse out of the river found the
body near the Argenteuil shore. Through one of their conscious instincts—namely shame—which governs women
even when they are in darkest despair, the sad victim had
carefully wrapped the seam of her dress around her feet.
This modest precaution was evidence that she had committed suicide. She was hardly disfigured when the sailors
brought her to the morgue. Her beauty, her youth, her rich
attire, her despair, occasioned a thousand speculations
about the cause of this catastrophe. The despair of her husband, the first to identify her, was boundless. He did not
understand this disaster, at least so I was told: I had not yet
seen the man. I told the Creole that the claims of the husband had priority. He had ordered a magnificent marble
tomb to hold the remains of his wife.

"After he killed her, the monster," screamed the Creole,
as he ran off enraged.

After the excitement, the despair of this young man,
after his fervent supplications to grant his wishes, after
his tears, I believed I could assume that he loved her and I
told him so. He confessed his love, but with the most
vivid protestations that his sister-in-law never knew of
this. He swore to it. Only to save his sister-in-law's repu-
tation, whose suicide public opinion would, as usual,
ascribe to some intrigue, did he want to shed light upon
the barbarity of his brother, even if thereby he were to

---

* and as soon as we were alone, he unveiled to me one of these wounds
that leaves incurable ulcers upon one's private life.

place himself on the accuser's bench. He begged me for my support.

What I could ascertain from his disconnected, passionate description is as follows: M. de M., his brother, was rich and a connoisseur of the arts, a lover of high living and high society. He had married this young woman about one year before. It seemed to have been mutual attraction; they were the loveliest pair imaginable. After the wedding, the bridegroom suddenly and strikingly began showing unmistakable signs of a possibly hereditary blood defect. This man, formerly so proud of his handsome appearance, his elegant figure in matchless perfection of form,[*] suddenly fell victim to an unknown evil against whose devastation science was powerless. He was terribly transformed from head to toe. He had lost all his hair; his spine had become bent. Most noticeable were the day-to-day changes in his appearance as he became thinner and more wrinkled. At least this was so to others; his vanity sought to deny the obvious to himself. None of this made him bedridden. An iron will seemed to overcome the attacks of this evil. Forcefully, he overcame the wreckage. His body fell in ruins, but his spirit soared. He continued organizing celebrations, overseeing hunting parties, continuing to live the life of wealth and splendor. It seemed to be built into his character and his nature. Yet, when he exercised his horse on the bridle paths, there were insults and innuendos, jokes by schoolboys and street children. There were rude and scornful smiles. The well-intentioned warnings by his friends about the frequent ridicule he was subjecting himself to by his fixation on gallant manners with the ladies, finally dissolved his illusions and caused him to be on his guard toward himself. As soon as he acknowledged his ugliness and deformity, as soon as

---

[*] Peuchet adds, after "form": "which meant that he had nothing to fear from rivals."

he became conscious thereof, his character turned embittered and cowardice descended upon him.

He seemed less eager to take his wife to soirées, balls, and concerts. He fled to his country home, ceased issuing any invitations, avoided people with a thousand excuses. So long as his pride gave him assurance of his superiority, he indulged his wife the attention she got from his friends. Now they made him jealous, suspicious, and violent. He saw in all those who persisted in visiting him the determination of making his wife's heart surrender, she who was his last source of pride and his last consolation. At this time the Creole arrived from Martinique on business, the success of which seemed to benefit from the reinstatement of the Bourbons to the French throne. His sister-in-law welcomed him superbly. In the course of the many connections that she arranged for him, the new arrival had the advantages to which his status as M. de M's brother naturally entitled him. Our Creole foresaw the isolation of the household that was developing, stemming not only from the direct quarrels his brother had provoked with numerous friends, but also from the thousand occurrences by which visitors were driven away and discouraged. Without very much taking into account the amorous motives which made him also jealous, the Creole supported these ideas of isolation and furthered them himself through his advice. M. de M. concluded the process by completely withdrawing to a lovely house in Passy that, in short order, became a desert. The slightest thing will stir jealousy. When it does not know where to turn, it feeds on itself and becomes inventive—everything nourishes it. Perhaps the young woman yearned for the pleasures suited to her age. Walls cut off the view of the neighbors' houses, and the shutters were closed from dawn to dusk.

The unfortunate woman was condemned to unbearable slavery and M. de M. exercised his slaveholding rights, sup-

ported by the civil code and the right of property. These
were based on social conditions which deem love to be
unrelated to the spontaneous feelings of the lovers, but
which permit the jealous husband to fetter his wife in
chains, like a miser with his hoard of gold, for she is but a
part of his inventory. M. de M., weapon in hand, strode
around the house at night, and made his rounds with dogs.
He imagined finding tracks in the sand. He lost himself in
strange assumptions about the placement of a ladder, which
a gardener had moved. The gardener himself, an almost 60-
year-old drunkard, was placed as a guard at the door. The
spirit of exclusion knows no limits to its excesses, it
extends to absurdity. The brother, an innocent accomplice
in all this, finally understood that he was collaborating in
the young woman's misfortune.

Day after day she was watched and insulted. It robbed
her of all that might have helped distract her through her
rich and happy imagination. She became gloomy and
melancholy, where before she had been free and cheerful.
She cried and hid her tears, but their traces were there to
read. The Creole became remorseful. He decided to declare
himself openly to his sister-in-law and to rectify his error,
which surely stemmed from his secret feelings of love. One
morning he crept into a little grove where the prisoner
occasionally came to get some air and look after her flowers. Even in this circumscribed freedom, one has to believe,
she knew she would be under the watchful eye of her jealous husband.

For at the sight of her brother-in-law, who at first
appeared before her unexpectedly, she became greatly agi-
tated and wrung her hands. "For God's sake, leave!" she
cried in a panic. "Leave." And indeed, he had hardly hidden
himself in a greenhouse, when M. de M. suddenly appeared.
The Creole heard screams. He wanted to eavesdrop, but the
pounding of his heart prevented his recourse to even the

smallest word of explanation of this escapade, which, if discovered by the husband could result in a lamentable outcome.

This event spurred on the brother-in-law; from this day
on he saw the necessity of becoming the victim's protector.
He forced himself to give up hidden thoughts of love.[*] Love
can sacrifice anything except its right to protect, for this
last sacrifice would be cowardice. He continued to visit his
brother, prepared to talk openly with him, to tell him all, to
expose himself. M. de M. had no suspicion of this aspect,
but his brother's persistence let it arise. Without clearly
reading the cause of his brother's interest, M. de M. mis-
trusted him, sensing in advance where it might lead.

The Creole soon realized that when he came to ring the
bell at the gate to the house in Passy and received no
answer, his brother was by no means always absent, as he
subsequently claimed. A journeyman locksmith made him
keys, copied from the models his master[†] had used for M.
de M.[‡] After ten days absence,[§] the Creole, embittered by
fear, and tortured by wild fantasies, climbed over the walls
one night, broke the gate to the main courtyard, and, with
a ladder, climbed up to the roof. Sliding down a drainpipe,
he reached a garret window.[‖] Loud cries induced him to
sneak, unnoticed, to a glass door. What he saw broke his
heart.

A lamp brightly lit the alcove. Beneath the draperies, his
hair in disarray, his face purple with rage, a half-naked M.
de M., on his knees near his wife on the same bed, show-
ered biting reproaches on his wife who cowered, not daring

[*] resolving to devote himself to his sister-in-law
[†] in Peuchet: "bourgeois" (boss)
[‡] The Creole was not afraid of the guard dogs; they knew him.
[§] a clever trick on the husband
[‖] near the bedroom of his brother-in-law [sic]

to move, yet trying half-heartedly to extricate herself. He was like a tiger, ready to tear her to pieces.

"Yes," he said to her, "I am ugly. I am a monster as I know only too well. I scare you. You wish to be freed from me, never again to be burdened with the sight of me. You long for the moment that will make you free of me. And, do not tell me the opposite. I can read your thoughts in your fear and your repugnance.* You blush at the undignified laughter that I arouse. Deep down, I revolt you. Surely you are counting every minute that has yet to pass until I shall no longer burden you with my infirmities and my presence. Stop! I am filled with horrible desires, a rage to disfigure you, to make you resemble me. Then you would no longer have the hope of solace from lovers for having the misfortune to have known me. I will shatter every mirror in this house, so that they will no longer reprove me with the contrast, will no longer serve to nourish your pride. Must I take or let you go out into the world so all can encourage you to hate me? No, no, you shall not leave this house until you have killed me. Kill me; do it, that which I have been daily tempted to do."[†]

With loud cries, with gnashing of teeth, with spittle on his lips, with a thousand symptoms of madness, with enraged self-inflicted blows, the wild man threw himself on the bed near his unhappy wife. She wasted tender caresses as well as pathetic entreaties on him. Finally she tamed him. Pity had, undoubtedly, replaced love, but that was not enough for this now revolting man, whose passions still retained so much energy. A prolonged feeling of dejection followed this scene, which turned the Creole cold as stone. He shuddered and knew not whom to turn to, to free the unfortunate woman from this **deadly** torment.

---

* and in your tears
[†] Kill me.

Apparently this scene was being repeated daily. To allay the spasms that followed these scenes, Mme. de M. took refuge in the medicine bottles, prepared for the purpose of affording her tormentor some peace.

At this time the Creole was the sole representative of the family in Paris. Perhaps he foresaw that starting legal proceedings would be risky. It is above all in these cases that one wants to curse the law's delays and its indifference. It cannot budge from its narrow, humdrum way, particularly when it is a question regarding a mere woman, the creature to whom the legislator provides the least protection. Only an arrest warrant or an arbitrator's act might have forestalled the tragedy that the witness to this madness foresaw. Nevertheless, he decided to risk all, to accept the costs of his decisions as his fortune enabled him and to make enormous sacrifices, not fearing for the accountability for his bold undertaking. Some physician friends of his, similarly determined, planned to break into M. de M.'s house to confirm the episodes of insanity and to separate the couple forcefully, when the occurrence of the suicide justified the too-long-delayed preparations and ended the problem.

Surely, for anyone who does not reduce to its literal meaning the whole spirit of a word, this suicide was an assassination perpetrated by the husband, but it was also the result of an intoxication of jealousy. The jealous man requires a slave he can love, but that love is only a handmaiden for his jealousy. *Above all, the jealous man is a private property owner.* *

---

* These last two sentences are almost entirely taken from another passage of Peuchet (see p. 130), which Marx substitutes for the following: "The unhappy husband, who survived his wife but a short time, was only evading his brother's accusation and profiting from the leniency of our laws, thanks to the excess of that very feeling which made him guilty. We determined correctly that this case would lead no further. If not to give him peace, at least."

I prevented the Creole from creating a useless and dangerous scandal, primarily endangering the memory of his beloved, as the idle public would have accused the victim of an adulterous relationship with the husband's brother.* I witnessed the funeral.[†] None but the brother and I knew the truth.[‡] Around me I heard unworthy mumblings about the suicide, and I regarded them with contempt. One blushes at public opinion when one observes it close at hand, with its cowardly malice and its salacious inferences. Opinion is too divided through the isolation of the people, too ignorant, too corrupt, for all are strangers to themselves and to one another.[§]

Few weeks passed, by the way, without bringing me similar revelations. That same year I recorded love matches that ended in two pistol shots, occasioned by the refusal of parents to grant their consent.

I also recorded suicides by men of the world, reduced to impotence in the bloom of their youth, having been plunged into uncontrollable melancholy by the abuse of pleasures.

Many people end their days subject to this obsession. Medicine, after long, unnecessary torment through ruinous prescriptions, could not free them from their miseries.

One could compile a strange collection of quotations from famous authors and poets which the despairing have written, preparing for their death with a certain splendor. During the moment of wonderful cold-bloodedness that

---

* The body was surrendered to M. de M., whose pain was the talk of our city, as exposed by a tearful scene in the cemetery of Montmartre as the priest was throwing the last ashes on the coffin.

[†] and a reproach died in my throat.

[‡] and even the guilty person seemed to be unaware of this fact, as was everyone else, blinded as he was by his own love for the victim.

[§] This last sentence, except for the concluding phrase, was taken from another passage by Peuchet (see p. 136).

comes with the decision to die, breathes a kind of conta-
gious inspiration that flows from these souls onto these
pages, even among those classes who were deprived of education. As they gather themselves together before the sacrifice, whose depths they have plumbed, they summon up all
their powers and, with characteristic, warm expression,
bleed to death.

Some of these poems, now buried in the archives, are
masterpieces. A dull bourgeois, who places his soul in his
business and his God in commerce, can find all this to be
very romantic and refute the pain that he cannot understand with derisive laughter. We are not surprised by his
derision. **What else to expect from three-percenters, who
have no inkling that daily, hourly, bit by bit, they kill themselves, their human nature.** But, what is one to say of those
good people who play the devout, **the educated,** and still
repeat this nastiness?

Undoubtedly, it is of great importance that the poor dev-
ils endure life, if only in the interest of the privileged
classes of this world who would be ruined by the large scale
suicide of this rabble. But, is there no other way to make
the existence of this class bearable besides insult, derisive
laughter, and beautiful words? Above all, there must exist a
kind of greatness of soul in these beggars who, fixed on
death as they are,* destroy themselves rather than choosing
the detour of the scaffold on the way to suicide. It is true
that **the more progress our economy makes,**† the more
rarely do these noble suicides occur, and conscious hostil-
ity takes its place and the unfortunate recklessly chance
robbery and murder. It is easier to get the death penalty
than to get work.

In rummaging through the police archives, I found

---

* are doing themselves in without looking for other solutions.
† in Peuchet: "in times of lack of faith."

only a single obvious symptom of cowardice among the list of suicides. It was the case of a young American, Wilfred Ramsay, who killed himself in order not to have to duel.*

The classification of the different causes of suicide would be the *classification of the failures of our society itself.*† One has killed oneself because some schemer stole one's invention, on which occasion the inventor plunged into the most awful misery due to the long, learned investigation to which he had to submit, without even being able to buy a legal brief. One has killed oneself to avoid the enormous cost and the demeaning persecution in financial difficulties, which have become so common, by the way, that those men mandated to administer the public weal pay no attention whatsoever. One has killed oneself because one cannot find work, after having groaned for a long time under the insults and the stinginess of those among us who are the arbitrary distributors of work.‡14

---

* He had been slapped with a glove by an elite guardsman at a public ball. His vindication was published in a newspaper of the time by a Quaker. I kept it but cannot find it. His defender then accused him a second time, reproaching him for not having nobly born the weight of the affront. (Editors' note: Evidently the Quaker applauded, out of pacifism, Ramsay's refusal to fight, but then attacked him for doing violence to himself after the suicide was reported.)

† My purpose is not to devote myself to this difficult type of analysis, which the legislator must enter upon, however, if he wants to extirpate completely from our soil the germs of dissolution wherein our generation grows and perishes as if it were being suffocated by an overgrowth of ivy.

‡ Our own secondary and social providence, the law, has a bloody debt toward God, its first legislator, as well as ours, for all that results in physical miseries, sufferings of the soul, and the cares of the mind. One will never reconcile oneself with the living by insulting the dead.

[Next Marx deleted two long case histories (see p. 120 in Peuchet). We briefly summarize them in note number 14—EDS.]

A physician consulted me one day regarding a death* for which he accused himself of being responsible.† One evening, on his return to Belleville, where he lived on a small street, he was stopped by a darkly veiled woman. In a trembling voice she begged him to listen to her. At some distance a person, whose features could not be discerned, was pacing up and down. She was being watched over by a man.‡

"Sir," she said to him, "I am pregnant and if this is discovered I will be dishonored. My family, the opinion of the world, the people of honor would not forgive me. The woman whose trust I have betrayed would go mad and would certainly divorce her husband. I do not defend my actions. I stand in the midst of a scandal whose eruption only my death can prevent. I wish to kill myself; others want me to live. I have been told that you are a compassionate man and this convinced me that you will not be an accomplice to the murder of a child, even an unborn one. You see, it is a question of an abortion. I will not lower myself to pleading or to the glossing over of that which I consider the most despicable of crimes. I'm giving in to the request **of strangers,** as I present myself to you, as I shall know how to die. I invoke death and for that I need nobody. One gives the appearance of finding pleasure in watering a garden; one puts on wooden shoes; one chooses a watery place, where one draws water every day; one arranges to disappear in the pool of the spring; and people will say it was a 'misfortune.'§ I have foreseen everything. Sir. I wish it

---

* of which I advised him (which he did) to leave all causes in the dark, although he thought it necessary to submit to men of heart and wisdom the questions that such a death too often triggers.

† And I leave it to fastidious consciences to decide if this man was really to blame. His scruples bothered me and raised scruples in me in turn.

‡ In Peuchet: "a gentleman."

§ Quotation marks added by Marx.

were the next morning, for I would go with all my heart. All is prepared, so that it will be so. But I was told to tell you and so I tell you. You must decide whether there are to be two murders or one. Out of my cowardice I have sworn an oath that I will abide by your decision without hesitation. Decide!"

"This alternative appalled me," the doctor continued, "the woman's voice rang pure and harmonious. Her hand which I held in mine was fine and delicate. Her free and unequivocal despair bespoke a fine sensibility. But, an issue that really made me shudder was at hand. Although in a thousand cases, for example in difficult deliveries when the surgical choice hovers between saving the mother and saving the child, politics or humanity decide the issue accordingly without scruple."

"Escape abroad," I said.

"Impossible," she responded. "It is unthinkable."

"Take clever precautions."

"I can't; I sleep in the same alcove with the woman whose friendship I betrayed."

"Is she a relative?"

"I may tell you no more."

"I would have given my life's blood," the doctor continued, "in order to save this woman from suicide or crime, or so that she could be freed from this conflict, without needing me. I accused myself of barbarity, for I shrank in dread from being an accessory to murder. It was a frightful struggle. Then a demon whispered to me that one doesn't necessarily kill oneself just because one really wants to die; that, by taking away their power to do harm, one forces these compromised people to renounce their vices."

I inferred luxury from the embroideries moving beneath her fingers and the resources of wealth in the elegant turn of her speech. One believes one owes the wealthy less sympathy; self-esteem aroused indignation against the thought of being seduced by the compensation of gold, although this matter had not been touched upon up to now. That was a matter of tact and evidence of respect for my character. I gave a negative response; the lady removed herself quickly. The sound of a carriage convinced me that I could never undo the harm I had done.

A fortnight later the newspapers brought the solution to the mystery.* The young niece of a Parisian banker, at most eighteen years old, the beloved ward of her aunt who had not let her out of her sight since the death of the girl's mother, had slipped and drowned in a stream on her guardian's estate near Villemomble. Her guardian was[†] inconsolable; in his role as uncle, he, the cowardly seducer, let himself be overcome by his sorrow before the world.[‡]

One sees that, for want of anything better, suicide becomes the most extreme refuge from the evils of private life.[§]

Among the causes of suicide I very frequently found dismissal from office, refusal of work, and a sudden drop in income, in consequence of which these families could no longer obtain the necessities of life, all the more so since most of them lived from hand to mouth.

At the time when one reduced the royal guards, a good man was fired, without ceremony, like all the rest.[‖] His age

---

* In Peuchet: "frightful doubt."

† In Peuchet: "guardians were."

‡ But I, I had killed the mother, while trying to save the child.

§ Should I now quote the example of a certain child, who, having been locked in the attic due to his father's anger, jumped in a frenetic rage from the sixth story of a building while among relatives? Should I also quote the examples of these unfortunates who each year asphyxiate themselves along with their children to escape poverty?

Let me close this sad chapter in which the evil that attacks all classes of society is so strongly put forth. One must be right in a measured way.

‖ Representative governments do not examine the situation closely. One takes into account the general economy; too bad about the detailed events.

and his lack of patronage precluded his transfer back to the army; his ignorance closed industry to him. He sought to enter the civil service but competitors,* numerous here as everywhere, blocked his way. He fell into heavy sorrow and killed himself. In his pocket one found a letter and disclosures of his circumstances. His wife was a poor seamstress; their two daughters, ages 16 and 18, worked with her. Tarnau, our suicide, wrote in the papers he left behind "that, since he could no longer be useful to his family and was forced to live as a burden to his wife and children, he saw it as his duty to take his life and free them from this added burden. He recommended his children to the Duchess of Angoulême.[15] He hoped that the goodness of this princess would take pity on so much misery." I drafted a report for the police prefect Angles and, after the necessary formalities, the Duchess provided 600 francs for the unfortunate family.†

Sad help, without doubt, after such a loss! But, how should one‡ family aid all the unfortunates since, when all is said and done, all France as it currently is, could not nourish them. The charity of the rich would not suffice even if our whole nation were religious, which it is far from being. ***Suicide reduces the most violent share of the difficulty, the scaffold the rest. Only by completely recasting our entire system of agriculture and industry can sources of income and true wealth be anticipated.*** It is easy to proclaim constitutions on parchment guaranteeing every citizen's right to education, to work, and, above all, to a mini-

---

* In Peuchet: "applicants."

† A note was given to the viscount of Montmorency, knight of Her Royal Highness. Madame gave orders that 600 FF be given to the unhappy Tarnau family. M. Bastien Beaupré, police chief of the district, was ordered to deliver this benefit.

‡ In Peuchet: "the royal."

mum subsistence-level existence. But it is not enough to put these magnanimous wishes on paper; there remains the essential task of bringing these liberal ideas to fruition through material and intelligent **social** institutions.

The ancient world of paganism brought splendid creations to this earth; will modern freedom* be left behind by her rivals? Who will join together these grandiose elements of power?†

Thus far Peuchet.

Finally, we want to present one of his tables on the annual incidence of suicide in Paris. From another table given by Peuchet, we learn that from 1817 to 1824 (inclusive), 2,808 suicides occurred in Paris. The number is of course greater in reality. Especially among the drowned, whose corpses are laid out in the morgue, one only knows in the rarest instances whether or not they were suicides.[16]

* this daughter of Christ,

†In order to get reliable data on suicide, I formed the plan for a big task. I first made an analytic and synthetic summary of police reports on suicide, then all data were input on tables with several columns on which were entered all peculiar characteristics as follows:

1. date of the event
2. person's name
3. his sex
4. civil status or profession
5. if the victim was married, with or without children
6. type of death or technique used to kill himself

In the seventh column, I put down various observations which could be drawn from the details in the other columns.

I narrowed my focus to three years: 1820, 1821, and 1824, as well as to the district of Paris. I believed that these three years would offer sufficient comparative information concerning the numbers and the known motives for committing suicide. To these I will add the data corresponding to the years 1817 to 1824.

Table of Suicides in Paris in the Year 1824

Number

1st semester	198
2nd semester	173
TOTAL	371

Outcome of suicide attempts

Survived	125
Not Survived	246
Males	239
Females	132
Unmarried	207
Married	164

Mode

Voluntary leap from heights	47
Strangulation	38
Knives	40
Firearms	42
Poisoning	28
Gas	61
Suffocation by voluntary leap into water	115

Motive

Disappointed love, family troubles	71
Sickness, weariness with life, imbecility	128
Bad conduct, gambling, lottery, fear of reproach and punishment	53
Misery, poverty, loss of position or work	59
Unknown motive	60

Notes

1. In keeping with previous English translations of Marx, we have rendered "Verkehr" as "intercourse," but in the nineteenth-century meaning of social contact—as in, for example, communication or trade relations—rather than its current primary meaning in English, sexual intercourse. We have also had to make choices in translating two words, each of them used frequently by Marx and Peuchet, that carry somewhat broader meanings in German or French than they do in English. Once again, we have tended to follow previous translations of Marx in this regard. One problem is that the German word *unglücklich* could be translated as "unfortunate," "unlucky," or "unhappy." Similarly, the French word *malheureux* could be translated as "unfortunate," "unhappy," or "wretched." We have usually rendered each of these as "unfortunate." A second problem occurs with the German word *Elend*, which could be translated as "misery" or "poverty," as could the French word *misère*. Here we have usually opted for "poverty."

2. Robert Owen (1771–1858) was a major British proponent of utopian socialism and of the cooperative movement. His New Lanark, Scotland, was a model factory town which both made a profit and provided generous social benefits to the workers, unheard of at the time. He was the author of *A New View of Society* (1813) and other works.

3. Charles Fourier (1772–1827) was an important French utopian socialist who championed women's rights and sexual freedom. He advocated model communities called phalastaneries in which property would be shared and individuals would work in a variety of occupations, rather than narrowly specializing. He was the author of *Theory of the Four Movements* (1808) and other works.

4. André Morellet (1727–1819), also known as Abbé Morellet, was a French theologian and philosopher. He worked on the core Enlightenment text the *Encyclopedia*, to which he contributed articles on religion. Imprisoned for two months in the Bastille in 1760 for his views, in 1762 he published *Manuel des Inquisitions*. Initially a supporter of the Revolution, he became disillusioned as early as August 1789 by the abolition of all feudal privileges. He also opposed the Jacobins but came back into prominence under Bonaparte's consulate in 1799, when he played a key role in the refounding of the Académie Française, of which he became a member.

5. The *Gazette de France*, a newspaper founded in 1631 with the support of Cardinal Richelieu, was devoted mainly to the reprinting of official documents and to foreign affairs. Up to 1789, it had a virtual monopoly on the publication of official and political information. After the Revolution,

it continued its monarchist orientation, appearing until 1915. Peuchet
served as editor during the years 1789 to 1790.

6. Mallet du Pan (1749–1800), a French writer and politician, was, along
with Edmund Burke and Joseph de Maistre, an important theorist of the con-
servative reaction to the French Revolution. Beginning in 1784, he was the
editor of *Mercure de France* (see note 7), a leading literary journal. In 1792,
he left the country at the behest of Louis XVI to contact other monarchs
opposed to the Revolution. His *Considérations sur la nature de la Révolution de France* (1793) drew wide attention in Europe for its critique of the
Revolution, and Mallet du Pan became a prominent adviser to those governments which opposed France. In 1797, he was forced to leave the conti-
nent for London, from where he began to publish *Le Mercure Britannique*.

7. *Mercure de France* was one of the country's first literary journals,
founded in 1672 as *Mercure galant*. It played a central part in debates over art
and culture until its demise in 1832. In 1790, after its editor, Mallet du Pan,
left France on a mission for King Louis XVI, Peuchet assumed the editorship,
which he held until 1792. During this period, *Mercure* vigorously defended
the King and the principles of monarchy against the revolutionaries. A new
Mercure de France was formed in 1890 by another group of intellectuals.

8. François de Neufchâteau (1750–1828), French poet and playwright,
took part in the early phases of the Revolution. He opposed the Jacobins,
which caused his arrest in 1793. In 1794, after their fall from power, he
resumed his political career, becoming Minister of the Interior in 1797. He
championed economic development, also founding the Louvre Museum.
From 1799–1815, under Bonaparte, he was a senator.

9. The Hundred Days, 20 March to 22 June 1815, a period in which
Napoleon returned from exile after his first defeat in 1814. He was restored
to power but exiled again permanently after the French defeat at Waterloo.

10. In fact, 1825.

11. The Constituent Assembly (1789–91) began the French Revolution
by promulgating the Declaration of the Rights of Man. It set up a new constitutional system which curbed the power of the monarchy and the
Catholic Church. The National Convention (1792–94) abolished the
monarchy and established the First Republic, but soon came under the dic-
tatorship of the Jacobin faction, which launched the Great Terror. The Tri-
bunate (1799–1807) was a legislative body under Bonaparte. Under the
Restoration, which began in 1814, the monarchy was returned to power
under Louis XVIII, and the Chamber of Deputies embarked on a series of
vengeful policies toward the Revolution and Bonaparte.

12. The exact title is *Statistique élémentaire de la France*, and the date
of publication was 1805, not 1807.

13. Germaine de Staël (1766–1817), known as Madame de Staël, was a leading French literary figure who maintained a famous Paris salon in the 1790s. Her literary and historical writings helped found Romanticism. A moderate liberal who advocated an English-style constitutional monarchy, she initially supported the Revolution, but from 1792 onward, she opposed successively the Jacobins, the Directory, and Bonaparte, which resulted in her frequent exile from France. Her writings include the novels *Delphine* (1802) and *Corinne* (1807) as well as political works such as *Considéra-tions sur la Révolution Française* (1818).

14. A woman and her daughter lived in poverty, ruined financially by the economic upheavals of the Bonapartist era. Following her mother's wishes, the daughter married a retired captain. The mother, however, who lived with them, sought to retain full power over her daughter, despite the latter's new status. The daughter's resistance led to open conflict. The husband was troubled by this but was afraid to intervene. Suddenly, domestic peace returned, and the daughter submitted once again to the mother's authority. The husband sought explanations but met a wall of silence from both women. Soon after, however, he unlocked a private chest where he discovered letters in the mother's possession indicating that the daughter had had sexual relations with three officers previous to the marriage. She had declared undying love to each of them, despite the embarrassingly close temporal proximity of these three sets of letters. Regardless of his view that such actions in one's past should be excused in a woman just as in a man, the husband said nothing about the apparent blackmailing of his wife by her mother. Soon the wife began to defy her mother's authority once again. At this point, the mother arranged, in an apparent escalation of her threats, to invite over for dinner the three officers with whom her daughter had been involved. Both husband and wife excused themselves from the dinner at the last minute but still did not communicate with each other about the source of the tension. The young wife disappeared that night. The next day her body was discovered underneath one of the bridges over the Seine. Peuchet used this vignette to comment on people's tendency to minimize or dismiss expressions of extreme despair in others. Our incredulity in the face of suicidal inclinations in others results, on the one hand, from social isolation and, on the other, from the morals of the epoch.

A young woman embroiderer, who has literary ambitions, marries a minor civil servant in 1814. Although she does not love him, she agrees to the marriage because a female friend convinces her that marrying this apparently upwardly mobile young man will improve her station in life. This same friend spreads far and wide the fact that their love is one sided, so much so that news of it reaches the groom just before the wedding. The bride reassures him, and the wedding goes forward. Almost immediately, however, the new husband becomes extremely jealous. The wife's attempts to placate him by complying with all his wishes only exacerbate his suspicions. By now, the young wife has dropped her literary efforts and, at the husband's urging, ceases to go out or to receive visitors in his absence. Distracted by his obsessive jealousy, the husband soon loses his job and begins to work only sporadically. The wife becomes worried about some Platonic but very warm letters which she exchanged with a young poet friend before the marriage. She recovers the letters but hesitates to burn them, hiding them instead. One day, her husband discovers the letters. When she refuses to let him see them, he seizes them by force. At this point, she threatens to leave him forever, or to drown herself, if he doesn't give them back immediately. Shaken, he gives her the letters, and leaves the house for a few minutes. Upon his return, he finds his wife gone and fragments of the burned letters fluttering in the fireplace. He promises himself to be more generous to his wife in the future, but it is too late. Distraught and contemplating suicide, the young wife has gone to visit one of her close female friends, but the friend is too busy with a guest from out of town to talk with her. Then, wandering the streets, she meets a very intelligent woman who tells her to return home, that her husband will probably take her back and apologize. The next day, with his wife still gone, the husband begins to tell people in their circle of acquaintances that he may physically attack the poet, accusing him publicly of seducing his wife. Two days later, the woman's body is found on the shore of an island in the Seine. She apparently took her life the very night she left home. Peuchet uses this vignette to discuss how unfeeling people are, how they gossip maliciously but fail to see what is really happening in other people's lives. They look for someone to blame rather than a true explanation of events.

Finally, in a much briefer passage, Peuchet recounts how suicides, once they are made public, can ruin the surviving families. In one case, a gunsmith who is facing bankruptcy shoots himself in the head late at night in his shop. Given the large quantity of gunpowder stored in the shop, the death might easily have been ruled an accident, but a chance witness hears the muffled shot and rouses the neighborhood. The suicide is discovered, and the family loses its inheritance. In other cases, people are found drowned, and the surviving families, denying suicidal intent, attribute the deaths to falling asleep or a careless accident. Later, suicide notes are found, and the families are dishonored. Peuchet uses this tale to illustrate how one cannot always easily determine how a death occurred. The implication is that there are more suicides than are recorded, a point Marx emphasizes in the last paragraph of his essay.

15. Marie-Thérèse, the Duchess of Angoulême (1778–1851), daughter of Louis XVI and Marie Antoinette, lived in exile until 1814, when she returned to France. She wielded great influence during the Restoration.

16. Marx omits five other annotated tables included by Peuchet at the end of his essay. Two of these tables, for 1820 and 1821, present the same types of data as those found in the 1824 table Marx reproduces. A third, very small table compares the number of suicides for 1820 and 1821. Another table presents data on attempted and completed suicides, and suicide by sex, for each of the years from 1817 to 1824. It is from this table that Marx derives the figure of 2,808 suicides, here merging both attempted and completed suicides, as Peuchet had done in his discussion. Also referring to this table, Peuchet discusses briefly the different levels of male and female suicides, since the number of male suicides was about double that of females for each of these years. He writes: "One will note here that the number of women is much less than that of men, whether because the women possess more courage in facing life's problems, a greater degree of resignation, or are sustained by a greater degree of religious sentiment; or whether, finally, and this appears most probable, their deep sorrow, by killing them, destroys their capacity to make a decision." Another table focuses on bodies found or people successfully rescued from bodies of water, and the sex of these people, for the years 1811–17. A final table gives data, also for 1811–17, on the number of bodies of suicide victims deposited at the Paris morgue, by sex and by where the body was found. One major problem with all these tables is that, although Peuchet presents his aggregate data by sex, he does not break down by sex his various subcategories, such as attempted versus successful suicides, causation, or the manner in which the suicide was carried out. But in pointing to these limitations, we also need to remember that these tables constitute a very early attempt to present social statistics.

Peuchet: vom Selbstmord

Karl Marx

Aus dem

GESELLSCHAFTSSPIEGEL

Organ zur Vertretung der besitzlosen Volksklassen und zur
Beleuchtung der gesellschaftlichen Zustände der Gegenwart
Zweiter Band
Elberfeld 1846

[Gesellschaftsspiegel. Bd. II. Heft VII. P. 14–26]

Die französische Kritik der Gesellschaft besitzt teilweise
wenigstens den großen Vorzug, die Widersprüche und die
Unnatur des modernen Lebens nicht nur an den Verhält-
nissen besondrer Klassen, sondern an allen Kreisen und
Gestaltungen des heutigen Verkehrs nachgewiesen zu
haben, und zwar in Darstellungen von einer unmittelbaren
Lebenswärme, reichhaltigen Anschauung, weltmännischer
Feinheit und geisteskühner Originalität, wie man sie bei
jeder andern Nation vergebens suchen wird. Man vergleiche
zum Beispiel die kritischen Darstellungen Owens und
Fouriers, soweit sie den lebendigen Verkehr betreffen, um
sich von dieser Überlegenheit der Franzosen eine Vorstel-
lung zu geben. Es sind keineswegs nur die eigentlich

„sozialistischen" Schriftsteller Frankreichs, bei denen man die kritische Darstellung der gesellschaftlichen Zustände suchen muß; es sind Schriftsteller aus jeder Sphäre der Literatur, namentlich aber der Roman und Memoirenliteratur. Ich werde in einigen Auszügen über den „Selbstmord" aus den „ mémoires tirés des archives de la police etc. par Jacques Peuchet" ein Beispiel dieser französischen Kritik geben, das zugleich zeigen mag, inwiefern die Einbildung der philanthropischen Bürger begründet ist, als ob es sich nur darum handle, den Proletariern etwas Brot und etwas Erziehung zu geben, als ob nur der Arbeiter unter dem heutigen Gesellschaftzustand verkümmere, im übrigen aber die bestehende Welt die beste Welt sei.

Bei Jacques Peuchet, wie bei vielen der ältern, jetzt fast ausgestorbenen französischen Praktiker, welche die zahlreichen Umwälzungen seit 1789, die zahlreichen Täuschungen, Begeisterungen, Konstitutionen, Herrscher, Niederlagen und Siege durchlebt haben erscheint die Kritik der bestehenden Eigentums-, Familien- und sonstigen Privat-Verhältnisse, mit einem Wort des Privatlebens, als das notwendige Ergebnis ihrer politischen Erfahrungen.

Jacques Peuchet (geboren 1760) ging von den schönen Wissenschaften zur Medizin, von der Medizin zur Jurisprudenz, von der Jurisprudenz zur Administration und dem Polizeifach über. Vor dem Ausbruch der französischen Revolution arbeitete er mit dem Abbé Morellet an einem dictionnaire du commerce, wovon indessen nur der Prospekt erschienen ist, und beschäftigte sich damals vorzugsweise mit der politischen Ökonomie und Administration. Nur sehr kurze Zeit war Peuchet ein Anhänger der französischen Revolution; er wandte sich sehr bald der royalistischen Partei zu, hatte eine Zeitlang die Hauptleitung der Gazette de France und übernahm sogar später von Mallet-du-Pan den berüchtigten royalistischen *Merkur.* Er wand sich indes höchst schlau durch die Revolution hindurch, bald verfolgt, bald im Departement der Administration und

1846.

Januar.

GESELLSCHAFTSSPIEGEL

Organ zur Vertretung der besitzlosen Volksklassen und zur Beleuchtung der gesellschaftlichen Zustände der Gegenwart

Heft VII.

Verlag von Julius Bädeker in Elberfeld.

Monatlich erscheint ein Heft. Der Preis des Jahrgangs von zwölf Heften ist in allen Buchhandlungen nur 2 Thlr., bei den preußischen Postämtern 2 Thlr. 10 Sgr. — ☞ Einzelne Hefte sind à 7½ Sgr. in allen Buchhandlungen zu haben.

der Polizei beschäftigt. Die von ihm 1800 publizierte Géographie commerçante, 5 Vol. in folio, zog die Aufmerksamkeit Bonapartes, des ersten Konsuls, auf ihn, er wurde zum membre du Conseil de commerce et des arts ernannt. Später nahm er unter dem Ministerium von François von Neufchâteau eine höhere Verwaltungsstelle ein. 1814 machte ihn die Restauration zum Zensor. Während der 100 Tage zog er sich zurück. Bei der Wiedereinsetzung der Bourbonen erhielt er den Posten eines Archivbewahrers der Polizeipräfektur zu Paris, den er bis 1827 bekleidete. Peuchet war direkt und als Schriftsteller nicht ohne Einfluß auf die Redner der Konstituante, des Konvents, des Tribunats, wie der Deputiertenkammern unter der Restauration. Unter seinen vielen meist ökonomischen Werken ist außer der schon zitierten Handelsgeographie seine Statistik von Frankreich (1807) das bekannteste.

Peuchet verfaßte seine Memoiren, deren Stoff er teils aus den Polizeiarchiven von Paris, teils aus seinen langen praktischen Erfahrungen in Polizei und Administration gesammelt hatte, als *Greis* und ließ sie erst erscheinen *nach seinem Tode,* so daß man ihn auf keinen Fall zu den „*voreiligen*" Sozialisten und Kommunisten zählen kann, denen die wunderbare Gründlichkeit und die allumfassenden Kenntnisse des großen Mittelschlags unserer Schriftsteller, Beamten und praktischen Bürger bekanntermaßen so vollständig abgehen.

Hören wir unsern Archivbewahrer der Polizeipräfektur zu Paris über den *Selbstmord!*

Die jährliche Zahl der Selbstmorde, die gewissermaßen normal und periodisch unter uns ist, muß betrachtet werden als ein Symptom der mangelhaften Organisation unserer Gesellschaft; denn zur Zeit des Stillstandes der Industrie und ihrer Krisen, in Epochen teurer Lebensmittel und in harten Wintern ist dieses Symptom immer augenfälliger und nimmt einen epidemischen Charakter an. Die Prostitution und der Diebstahl wachsen dann in derselben Proportion. Obgleich das Elend die größte Quelle des Selbstmords ist, finden wir ihn wieder in allen Klassen, bei den müßigen Reichen, wie bei den Künstlern und Politikern. Die Verschiedenheit der Ursachen, die ihn motivieren, verspottet gleichsam den einfömigen und lieblosen Tadel der Moralisten.

Auszehrungskrankheiten, wogegen die gegenwärtige Wissenschaft träg und unzureichend ist, mißbrauchte Freundschaft, betrogne Liebe, entmutigter Ehrgeiz, Familienleiden, erstickter Wetteifer, Überdruß an einem monotonen

Leben, ein Enthusiasmus, der auf sich selbst zurückgedrängt ist, sind sehr sicher Veranlassungen des Selbstmordes für Naturen von reicherem Umfang, und die Liebe des Lebens selbst, diese energische Schwungkraft der Persönlichkeit, führt sehr oft dazu, sich loszumachen von einer verabscheuungswürdigen Existenz.

Frau von Staël, deren größtes Verdienst darin besteht, Gemeinplätze glänzend stilisiert zu haben, hat zu zeigen versucht, daß der Selbstmord eine widernatürliche Handlung ist, und daß man ihn nicht als eine Tat des Mutes betrachten könne; sie hat vor allem aufgestellt, daß es würdiger sei, gegen die Verzweiflung zu kämpfen, als ihr zu unterliegen. Derartige Gründe affizieren wenig die Seelen, welche das Unglück überwältigt. Sind sie religiös, so spekulieren sie auf eine bessere Welt; glauben sie dagegen an Nichts, so suchen sie die Ruhe des Nichts. Die philosophischen Tiraden haben in ihren Augen keinen Wert und sind eine schwache Zuflucht gegen das Leiden. Es ist vor allem abgeschmackt, zu behaupten, daß eine Handlung, die sich so oft vollzieht, eine widernatürliche Handlung sei; der Selbstmord ist in keiner Weise widernatürlich, weil wir täglich seine Zeugen sind. Was gegen die Natur ist, ereignet sich nicht. Es liegt im Gegenteil *in der Natur unsrer Gesellschaft*, viele Selbstmorde zu gebären, während die Tartaren sich nicht selbst morden. *Alle Gesellschaften haben also nicht dieselben Produkte*, das ist's, was man sich sagen muß, um an der Reform der unsrigen zu arbeiten und sie eine höhere Stufe erklimmen zu lassen. Was den Mut betrifft, wenn man für mutig passiert, sobald man dem Tod trotzt am hellen Tag auf dem Schlachtfeld unter der Herrshaft aller vereinigten Aufregungen, so beweist nichts, daß man notwendig seiner entbehrt, wenn man sich selbst und in finstrer Einsamkeit den Tod gibt. Man durchhaut eine solche Streitfrage nicht durch Insulte gegen die Toten.

Alles, was man gegen den Selbstmord gesagt hat, dreht sich in demselben Zirkel von Ideen herum. Man stellt ihm entgegen die Beschlüsse der Vorsehung, aber die Existenz des Selbstmordes selbst ist ein offener Protest gegen die unleserlichen Beschlüsse. Man spricht uns von unsern Pflichten gegen diese Gesellschaft, ohne unsre Rechte auf die Gesellschaft ihrerseits zu erklären und zu verwirklichen, und man exaltiert endlich das tausendmal größere Verdienst, den Schmerz zu überwältigen, als ihm zu unterliegen, ein Verdienst, eben so traurig, wie die Perspektive, die es eröffnet. Kurz man macht aus dem Selbstmord einen Akt der Feigheit, ein Verbrechen gegen die Gesetze, die Gesellschaft und die Ehre.

Woher kommt es, daß der Mensch trotz so vieler Anatheme sich solbst ermordet? Weil das Blut nicht in derselben Weise in den Adern verzweifelter Leute fließt, wie das Blut der kalten Wesen, die sich die Muße nehmen, alle diese unfruchtbaren Redensarten zu debütieren. *Der Mensch scheint ein Geheimnis für den Menschen; man weiß ihn nur zu tadeln und man kennt ihn nicht.* Wenn man sieht, wie leichtsinnig die Institutionen, unter deren Herrschaft Europa lebt, über Blut und Leben der Völker verfügen, wie sich die zivilisierte Justiz mit einem reichen Material von Gefängnissen, Züchtigungen, Todesinstrumenten für die Sanktion ihrer unsichern Beschlüsse umgibt; wenn man die unerhörte Zahl der Klassen sieht, die von allen Seiten im Elend gelassen werden, und die sozialen Parias, die man mit einer brutalen und präventiven Verachtung schlägt, vielleicht um sich der Mühe zu überheben, sie ihrem Schmutz zu entreißen; wenn man alles dies sieht, so begreift man nicht, infolge welchen Titels man dem Individuum befehlen kann, an sich selbst eine Existenz zu achten, die unsre Gewohnheiten, unsre Vorurteile, unsere Gesetze und unsre Sitten im allgemeinen mit Füßen treten.

Man hat geglaubt die Selbstmorde aufhalten zu können durch beschimpfende Strafen und durch eine Art von Infamie, mit der man das Andenken des Schuldigen brand-

markt. Was ist von der Unwürdigkeit einer Brandmarkung
zu sagen, geschleudert auf Leute, die nicht mehr da sind,
ihre Sache zu plädieren? Die Unglücklichen kümmen sich
übrigens wenig darum; und wenn der Selbstmord irgend
einen anklagt, sind es vor allem die Leute, die zurückbleiben, weil in dieser Masse nicht Einer verdient, daß man
für ihn leben blieb. Die kindischen und grausamen Mittel,
die man ersonnen hat, haben sie siegreich gekämpft gegen
die Zuflüsterungen der Verzweiflung? Was liegt dem
Wesen, welches die Welt fliehen will, an den Beleidigungen,
die die Welt seinem Leichnam verspricht? es sieht hierin
nur eine Feigheit mehr von Seite der Lebenden. *Was ist das
in der Tat für eine Gesellschaft, wo man die tiefste Einsamkeit im Schoß von mehreren Millionen findet; wo man
von einem unbezwingbaren Verlangen, sich selbst zu
töten, überwältigt werden kann, ohne daß irgend einer uns
errät! Diese Gesellschaft ist keine Gesellschaft, sie ist, wie
Rousseau sagt, eine Wüste, bevölkert mit wilden Tieren.* In
den Stellen, die ich bei der Administration der Polizei be-
kleidet habe, bildeten die Selbstmorde einen Teil meiner
Attributionen; ich wollte kennen lernen, ob in ihren be-stim-
menden Ursachen sich nicht einige finden würden, deren
Wirkung man zuvorkommen könnte. Ich hatte über diesen
Gegenstand eine umfassende Arbeit unternommen. Ich fand,
daß außer einer totalen Reform der jetzigen Gesellschaftsord-
nung alle andern Versuche vergeblich sein würden.

Unter den Ursachen der Verzweiflung, welche sehr
nervösreizbare Personen den Tod suchen lassen, leiden-
schaftliche und tieffühlende Wesen, habe ich als vor-
herrschende Tatsache die schlechte Behandlung entdeckt,
die Ungerechtigkeiten, die geheimen Strafen, welche
harte Eltern und Vorgesetzte die Personen, welche in ihrer
Abhängigkeit sind, erdulden lassen. *Die Revolution hat
nicht alle Tyranneien gestürzt; die Übel, die man den
willkürlichen Gewalten vorgeworfen hat, bestehen in den*

Familien; sie verursachen hier Krisen, analog denen der Revolutionen.

Die Verhälnisse zwischen den Interessen und den Gemütern, die wahren Beziehungen unter den Individuen sind *von Grund und Boden aus* erst unter uns zu schaffen und der *Selbstmord ist nur eins der tausend und ein Symptome des allgemeinen,* immer auf frischer Tat begriffenen *sozialen Kampfes,* wovon so viele Kämpfende sich zurück-ziehen, weil sie müde sind, unter den Opfern zu zählen, oder weil sie sich empören gegen den Gedanken, unter den Henkern eine Ehrenstufe einzunehmen. Will man einige Beispiele, ich will sie aus authentischen Protokollen ausziehen.

Im Monat Juli 1816 verlobte sich die Tochter eines Schneiders mit einem Schlächter, einem jungen Menschen von guten Sitten, ökonomisch und arbeitsam, sehr eingenommen von seiner schönen Braut, die ihrerseits wieder ihm sehr zugetan war. Das junge Mädchen war Nähterin; sie besaß die Achtung aller derer, die sie kannten, und die Eltern ihres Bräutigams liebten sie zärtlich. Diese braven Leute versäumten keine Gelegenheit, den Besitz ihrer Schwiegertochter zu antizipieren; man ersann Vergnügungspartien, deren Königin und Idol sie war.

Die Epoche der Heirat kam heran; alle Anordnungen unter den beiden Familien waren getroffen und die Verträge abgeschlossen. Den Abend des Tages, der festgesetzt war, um sich auf die Munizipalität zu begeben, sollten die junge Tochter und ihre Eltern bei der Familie des Bräutigams zu Abend essen; ein unbedeutender Vorfall kam unvermutet dazwischen. Aufträge, die für ein reiches Haus ihrer Kundschaft zu besorgen waren, hielten den Schneider und seine Frau in ihren Wohnungen zurück. Sie entschuldigten sich; aber die Mutter des Schlächters kam selbst, ihre Schwiegertochter abzuholen, welche die Erlaubnis erhielt, ihr zu folgen.

Trotz der Abwesenheit von zwei der Hauptgäste war das Mahl eins der heitersten. Viele der Familienscherze, welche die Aussicht auf eine Hochzeit autorisiert, wurden zum Besten gegeben. Man trank, man sang. Die Zukunft wurde auf das Tapet gebracht. Die Freuden einer guten Ehe wurden sehr lebhaft analysiert. Sehr spät in der Nacht fand man sich noch an der Tafel. Aus einer leicht erklärbaren Nachsicht schlossen die Eltern des jungen Menschen die Augen über das stillschweigende Einverständnis der beiden Verlobten. Die Hände suchten sich, die Liebe und die Vertraulichkeit stiegen ihnen in den Kopf. Überdem betrachtete man die Ehe als vollzogen, und diese jungen Leute hatten sich seit sehr langer Zeit besucht, ohne daß man den leisesten Vorwurf an sie richten konnte. Die Rührung der Eltern des Verlobten, die vorgerückte Stunde, die wechselseitigen, sehnsüchtigen Wünsche, entfesselt durch die Nachsicht ihrer Mentoren, die ungenierte Heiterkeit, die immer bei solchen Mahlen herrscht, alles dies vereinigt, und die Gelegenheit, die sich lächelnd anbot, und der Wein, der in den Köpfen sprudelte, alles begünstigte einen Ausgang, der sich ahnen läßt. Die Liebenden fanden sich wieder im Dunkel, nachdem die Lichter verglommen waren. Man stellte sich nichts zu merken, nichts zu ahnen. Ihr Glück hatte hier nur Freunde und keine Neider.

Die junge Tochter kehrte erst den andern Morgen zu ihren Eltern zurück. Ein Beweis, wie wenig schuldig sie sich zu sein glaubte, liegt schon darin, daß sie allein zurückkehrte. Sie schlich in ihre Kammer und machte ihre Toilette zurecht; aber kaum hatten ihre Eltern sie wahrgenommen, als sie ihre Tochter mit Wut mit den schändlichsten Namen und Schimpfreden überschütteten. Die Nachbarschaft war Zeuge davon, der Skandal hatte keine Grenzen. Urteilt von der Erschütterung dieses Kindes, durch ihre Scham und durch das Mysterium, das man schimpflich verletzte. Vergebens stellt das bestürzte Mädchen ihren Eltern vor, daß sie selbst sie in Verruf brächten, daß sie ihr Unrecht, ihre Torheit, ihren Ungehorsam eingestände, aber daß alles wieder gut gemacht werden würde. Ihre Gründe und ihr Schmerz entwaffneten nicht das Schneiderpaar. Die feigsten, widerstandsunfähigsten Menschen werden unerbittlich, sobald sie die *absolute elterliche Autorität geltend machen können. Der Mißbrauch derselben* ist gleichsam ein *roher Ersatz* für die viele Unterwürfigkeit und Abhängigkeit, denen sie sich in der bürgerlichen Gesellschaft mit oder wider Willen unterwerfen. Gevatter und Gevatterinnen kamen zu dem Lärm hinzugelaufen und machten Chorus. Das Gefühl der Scham, welches diese abscheuliche Szene hervorrief, brachte das Kind zu dem Entschluß, sich das Leben zu rauben; raschen Schrittes stieg sie herab, mitten durch die schimpfenden und fluchenden Gevattersleute, mit geistesirren Blicken, stürzte zur Seine und warf sich in den Fluß;—die Schiffsleute zogen sie tot aus dem Wasser, geziert mit ihrem Hochzeitsschmuck. Wie sich von selbst versteht, wandten sich die, welche im Anfang gegen die Tochter geschrien hatten, sogleich gegen die Eltern; diese Katastrophe erschreckte die nichtigen Seelen. Wenige Tage nachher kamen die Eltern auf die Polizei, um eine goldne Kette, welche das Kind an seinem Halse trug, ein Geschenk ihres künftigen Schwiegervaters, eine silberne Uhr und mehrere andre Kleinodien zu reklamieren, lauter Gegenstände, die in den Bureaus deponiert waren. Ich verfehlte nicht, mit Energie diesen Leuten ihre Unklugheit und Barbarei vorzuwerfen. Diesen Tollen sagten, daß sie vor Gott Rechenschaft ablegen müßten, das hätte in Anbetracht ihrer engherzigen Vorurteile und der eignen Art Religiosität, die in den niedern merkantilischen Klassen herrscht, sehr wenig Eindruck auf sie gemacht.

Die Habsucht zog sie herbei, nicht das Verlangen, zwei oder drei Reliquien zu besitzen; ich glaubte, sie durch ihre Habsucht bestrafen zu können. Sie reklamierten die Kleinodien ihrer jungen Tochter; ich verweigerte sie ihnen, ich behielt die Zertifikate, die sie bedurften, um diese Effekten von der Kasse zurück zu ziehen, wo man sie wie gebräuchlich deponiert hatte. So lange ich an diesem Posten war, waren ihre Reklamationen vergeblich und ich fand ein Vergnügen daran, ihren Injurien zu trotzen.

In demselben Jahre erschien in meinem Bureau ein junger Kreole, von einer reizenden Figur, aus einer der reichsten Familien Martiniques. Er widersetzte sich aufs förmlichste dagegen, daß man den Leichnam einer jungen Frau, seiner Schwägerin, dem Reklamanten, seinem eignen Bruder und ihrem Gemahl, zurükgebe. Sie hatte sich ertränkt. Diese Art Selbstmord ist die häufigste. Der Körper war von den zum Auffischen der Leichname angestellten Beamten nicht weit von der grève d'Argenteuil aufgefunden worden. Durch einen jener bewußten Instinkte der Scham, welcher die Frauen sogar in der blindesten Verzweiflung beherrscht, hatte sich die Ertrunkene den Saum ihres Kleides sorgsam um ihre Füße geschlungen. Diese verschämte Vorsicht bewies den Selbstmord bis zur Evidenz. Sie war sogleich, nachdem man sie aufgefunden, nach der Morgue gebracht worden. Ihre Schönheit, ihre Jugend, der reiche Anzug gaben Anlaß zu tausend Vermutungen über die Ursache dieser Katastrophe. Die Verzweiflung ihres Mannes, der sie zuerst erkannte, war grenzenlos; er begriff dies Unglück nicht, wenigstens wie man mir sagte; ich selbst hatte ihn nie früher gesehen. Ich stellte dem Kreolen vor, daß die Reklamation des Gatten allen andern vorgehe, der soeben ein prachtvolles Grabmal von Marmor für seine unglückliche Frau erbauen lasse. „Nachdem er sie getötet hat, das Ungeheuer!" schrie der Kreole, indem er mit Wut auf und ab lief.

Nach der Aufregung, der Verzweiflung dieses jungen Mannes, nach seinen flehentlichen Bitten, ihm seine Wünsche zu gewähren, nach seinen Tränen glaubte ich schließen zu können, daß er sie liebe, und ich sagte es ihm. Er gestand seine Liebe ein; aber unter den lebhaftesten

Beteurungen, daß seine Schwägerin nie etwas davon gewußt hätte. Er beschwor es. Nur um den Ruf seiner Schwägerin zu retten, deren Selbstmord die öffentliche Meinung wie gewöhnlich eine Intrige unterschieben werde, wolle er die Barbareien seines Bruders ans Licht ziehen, und sollte er sich selbst auf die Anklagebank setzen müssen. Er bat mich um meine Unterstützung. Was ich aus seinen abgebrochnen, leidenschaftlichen Erklärungen entnehmen konnte, war dies: Herr von M . . . ., sein Bruder, reich und kunstliebend, ein Freund des Luxus und hoher Zirkel, hatte sich seit einem Jahre ungefähr mit dieser jungen Frau verheiratet; wie es schien, aus gegenseitiger Neigung; sie waren das schönste Paar, das man sehen konnte. Nach der Heirat war in der Konstitution des jungen Ehegatten ein Fehler des Bluts, vielleicht ein Familienfehler, plötzlich und mit Heftigkeit ausgebrochen. Dieser Mann, früher so stolz auf sein schönes Äußere, seine elegante Tournüre, auf eine Vollendung, eine Vollkommenheit der Formen ohnegleichen, verfiel plötzlich einem unbekannten Übel, gegen dessen Verheerungen die Wissenschaft ohnmächtig war; er war von Kopf bis zu Fuß auf die entsetzlichste Weise umgestaltet. Er hatte alle seine Haare verloren, sein Rückgrat hatte sich gekrümmt. Von Tag zu Tag verwandelten ihn die Magerkeit und die Runzeln auf das auffallendste; für die andern wenigstens, denn seine Eigenliebe suchte das Augenscheinliche wegzuleugnen. Aber das alles machte ihn nicht bettlägerig; eine eiserne Stärke schien über die Angriffe dieses Übels zu triumphieren. Er überlebte kräftig seine eigenen Trümmer. Der Körper fiel in Ruinen und die Seele blieb oben auf. Er fuhr fort, Feste zu geben, Jagdpartien vorzustehn und die reiche und prunkvolle Lebensweise fortzuführen, die das Gesetz seines Charakters und seiner Natur schien. Jedoch die Beleidigungen, die Quodlibets, die Scherzworte der Schüler und Sraßenjungen, wenn er in den Promenaden sein Pferd tummelte, unhöfliches und spöttisches Lächeln, dienstfertige Warnungen von Freunden über die zahlreichen Ridicules, die er sich durch sein Versessensein auf galante Manieren bei den Damen gebe, lösten endlich seine Illusion auf und machten ihn gegen sich selbst vorsichtig. Sobald er sich seine Häßlichkeit und seine Mißgestalt eingestand, sobald er das Bewußtsein davon hatte, verbitterte sich sein Charakter, er ward kleinmütig. Er schien minder eifrig bemüht, seine Frau auf Soireen zu führen, auf Bälle, auf Konzerte; er flüchtete sich in seine Wohnung aufs Land; er machte allen Einladungen ein Ende, bog den Leuten unter tausend Vorwänden aus; und die Artigkeiten seiner Freunde gegen seine Frau, von ihm geduldet, so lange der Stolz ihm die Gewißheit seiner Überlegenheit gab, machten ihn eifersüchtig, argwöhnisch, heftig. Er sah in allen denen, welche darauf beharrten, ihn zu besuchen, den festen Entschluß, das Herz seiner Frau kapitulieren zu machen, die ihm als sein letzter Stolz und sein letzter Trost blieb. Um diese Zeit kam der Kreole von Martinique an, in Geschäften, deren Erfolg die Wiedereinsetzung der Bourbonen auf den französischen Thron zu begünstigen schien. Seine Schwägerin empfing ihn ausgezeichnet; und in dem Schiffbruche von zahllosen Verbindungen, die sie kontrahiert hatte, erhielt sich der neu Angekommene den Vorteil, den sein Titel als Bruder ihm ganz natürlich bei Herrn von M . . . . gab. Unser Kreole sah die Einsamkeit voraus, die sich um die Haushaltung bilden würde, sowohl aus den direkten Zänkereien, die sein Bruder mit mehreren Freunden hatte, als aus tausend indirekten Vorgängen, um die Besucher zu verjagen und zu entmutigen. Ohne sich gerade Rechenschaft abzulegen über die Liebesmotive, die ihn selbst eifersüchtig machten, billigte der Kreole diese Ideen der Absonderung und begünstigte sie selbst durch seine Ratschläge. Herr von M . . . . endigte damit, sich gänzlich in ein schönes Haus in Passy zurückzuziehen, das in kurzer Zeit eine Wüste wurde. Die

Eifersucht nährt sich von den geringsten Dingen, wenn sie nicht weiß, woran sich hängen, zehrt sie sich selbst auf und wird erfinderisch; alles dient ihr zur Nahrung. Vielleicht sehnte sich die junge Frau nach den Vergnügungen ihres Alters. Mauern fingen die Aussicht auf die benachbarten Wohnungen auf; die Läden waren von morgens bis abends geschlossen. Das unglückliche Weib war zur unerträglichsten Sklaverei verurteilt und diese Sklaverei übte Herr von M . . . . nur aus, gestützt auf den Code Civil und das Eigentumsrecht, gestützt auf einen gesellschaftlichen Zustand, der die Liebe unabhängig macht von den freien Empfindungen der Liebenden und dem eifersüchtigen Ehemann gestattet, seine Frau mit Schlössern zu umgeben, wie dem Geizhals seinen Geldkoffer; denn sie bildet nur einen Teil seines Inventariums. Herr von M . . . . strich mit Waffen während der Nacht um das Haus herum und machte seine Runde mit Hunden. Er bildete sich ein, Spuren auf dem Sand wahrzunehmen, und verirrte sich in seltsamen Voraussetzungen bei Gelegenheit einer Leiter, die ihren Platz durch den Gärtner gewechselt hatte. Der Gärtner selbst, ein fast 60jähriger Trunkenbold, wurde als Wache an das Tor gestellt. Der Geist der Ausschließung hat keinen Zügel in seinen Extravaganzen, er geht fort bis zur Albernheit. Der Bruder, unschuldiger Mitschuldiger von all diesem, begriff endlich, daß er am Unglück der jungen Frau arbeitete, welche von Tag zu Tag überwacht, insultiert, alles dessen beraubt, was eine reiche und glückliche Phantasie zerstreuen konnte, eben so finster und melancholisch wurde, als sie frei und heiter gewesen war. Sie weinte und verbarg ihre Tränen, aber deren Spur war leserlich. Gewissensbisse kamen dem Kreolen. Entschlossen, sich offen seiner Schwägerin zu erklären und einen Fehler wieder gut zu machen, der sicher aus einer verstohlenen Empfindung von Liebe hervorgegangen war, schlich er eines Morgens in ein Lustwäldchen, wo die Gefangene von Zeit zu Zeit Luft schöpfen und ihre Blumen besorgen ging. Beim Gebrauch dieser so beschränkten Freiheit wußte sie, man muß es glauben, daß sie unter dem Auge ihres eifersüchtigen Gemahls war; denn beim Anblick ihres Schwagers, der sich zum erstenmal und unvermutet ihr gegenüber befand, zeigte die junge Frau die größte Bestürzung, sie rang ihre Hände. ,,Entfernen Sie sich, im Namen des Himmels," rief sie ihm erschreckt zu. ,,Entfernen Sie sich!"

Und in der Tat, er hatte kaum die Zeit, sich in ein Treibhaus zu verbergen, als Herr von M. plötzlich erschien. Der Kreole hörte Geschrei, er wollte lauschen; das Schlagen seines Herzens verhinderte ihn, das leiseste Wort einer Erklärung zu verstehen, welcher diese Flucht, wenn der Gatte sie entdeckte, einen beweinenswerten Ausgang geben konnte. Dieser Vorfall spornte den Schwager an; er sah hier die Notwendigkeit, von diesem Tage an der Beschützer eines Opfers zu sein. Er entschloß sich, jedem verliebten Rückhalt zu entsagen. Die Liebe kann alles aufopfern, nur nicht ihr Protektoratsrecht, denn dieses letzte Opfer wäre das eines Feigen. Er fuhr fort, seinen Bruder zu besuchen, bereit, offen zu ihm zu sprechen, sich ihm zu enthüllen, ihm alles zu sagen. Herr von M. hatte noch keinen Verdacht von dieser Seite, aber diese Beharrlichkeit seines Bruders ließ ihn entstehen. Ohne ganz klar in den Ursachen dieses Interesses zu lesen, mißtraute Herr v. M. denselben, vorher berechnend, wozu es führen könne. Der Kreole sah bald ein, daß sein Bruder nicht immer abwesend war, wie er hinterher behauptete, so oft man vergeblich an das Tor des Hauses von Passy schellen kam. Ein Schlossergeselle machte ihm die Schlüssel nach dem Modell derer, die sein Meister für Herrn von M. geschmiedet hatte. Nach einer Entfernung von zehn Tagen drang der Kreole erbittert aus Furcht und gequält von den tollsten Chimären nachts über die Mauern ein, zerbrach ein Gitter vor dem Haupthof, erreichte das Dach vermittelst einer Leiter und ließ sich an der

Dachrinne hinabgleiten bis unter das Fenster eines Spei-
chers. Heftige Ausrufungen veranlaßten ihn, sich bis zu
einer Glastüre unbemerkt hinanzuschleichen. Was er sah,
zerriß sein Herz. Die Klarheit einer Lampe erleuchtete den
Alkoven. Unter den Vorhängen, die Haare in Unordnung
und das Gesicht purpurfarben vor Wut, überhäufte Herr von
M., halbnackt, niedergekauert in der Nähe seiner Frau, auf
dem Bette selbst, das sie nicht zu verlassen wagte, obgleich
sich ihm halb und halb entwindend, sie mit den beißend-
sten Vorwürfen und schien ein Tiger, bereit sie in Stücke zu
zerreißen. ,,Ja," sagte er zu ihr, ,,ich bin häßlich, ich bin ein
Ungeheuer und ich weiß es nur zu wohl, ich flöße dir
Furcht ein. Du wünschest, daß man dich von mir befreie,
daß mein Anblick dich nicht mehr belästige. Du verlangst
nach dem Augenblick, der dich frei machen wird. Und sage
mir nicht das Gegenteil; ich errate deine Gedanken in
deinem Schrecken, in deinem Widerstreben. Du errötest
über das unwürdige Gelächter, das ich errege, du bist inner-
lich empört gegen mich! Du zählst ohne Zweifel eine nach
der andern die Minuten, die verfließen müssen, bis ich dich
nicht mehr mit meinen Schwächen und meiner Gegenwart
belagere. Halt! es ergreifen mich entsetzliche Wünsche, die
Wut, dich zu entstellen, dich mir ähnlich zu machen, damit
du nicht die Hoffnung behalten kannst, dich mit Lieb-
habern über das Unglück zu trösten, mich gekannt zu
haben. Ich werde alle Spiegel dieses Hauses entzweischla-
gen, damit sie mir keinen Kontrast vorwerfen, damit sie
aufhören, deinem Stolz zur Nahrung zu dienen. Nicht
wahr, ich müßte dich in die Welt führen, oder dich dahin
gehn lassen, um zu sehen, wie jeder dich ermuntert mich
zu hassen? Nein, nein, du wirst dies Haus nicht verlassen,
ehe du mich getötet hast. Töte mich, komme dem zuvor,
was ich versucht bin, alle Tage zu tun!" Und der Wilde
wältzte sich auf dem Bett mit lautem Geschrei, mit Zähne-
fletschen, den Schaum auf den Lippen, mit tausend Symp-

tomen der Raserei, mit Schlägen, die er sich selbst in seiner Wut beibrachte, in der Nähe dieser unglücklichen Frau, die die zartesten Liebkosungen an ihn verschwendete und das pathetischste Flehen. Endlich zähmte sie ihn. Das Mitleid hatte ohne Zweifel die Liebe ersetzt; aber das genügte nicht diesem so abschreckend gewordenen Mann, dessen Leidenschaften noch so viel Energie bewahrt hatten. Eine lange Niedergeschlagenheit war die Folge dieser Szene, die den Kreolen versteinerte. Er schauderte und wußte nicht, an wen sich wenden, um die Unglückliche dieser Todesmarter zu entreißen. Diese Szene mußte sich offenbar alle Tage wiederholen, denn in den Krämpfen, die ihr folgten, nahm Frau von M. ihre Zuflucht zu Arzneiflaschen, die zu dem Zweck präpariert waren, ihrem Henker ein wenig Ruhe wieder zu geben. Der Kreole repräsentierte zu Paris in diesem Augenblick allein die Familie des Herrn von M. Es ist in diesen Fällen vor allen, wo man die Langsamkeit der gerichtlichen Formen verfluchen möchte und die Sorglosigkeit der Gesetze, die nichts aus ihrem abgezirkelten Schlendrian heraustreiben kann, namentlich da es sich nur um eine Frau handelte, das Wesen, welches der Gesetzgeber mit den mindesten Garantien umgibt. Ein Verhaftbefehl, eine willkürliche Maßregel wären allein dem Unglück zuvorgekommen, welches der Zeuge dieser Raserei zu wohl vorhersah. Er entschloß sich jedoch alles für alles zu wagen, alle Folgen auf seine Rechnung zu nehmen, indem sein Vermögen ihn befähigte, enorme Opfer zu bringen und die Verantwortlichkeit keines Wagestücks zu fürchten. Schon bereiteten einige Ärzte unter seinen Freunden, entschlossen wie er selbst, einen Einfall in das Haus des Hrn. von M. vor, um diese Momente des Wahnsinns zu konstatieren und durch unmittelbare Gewalt die beiden Gatten zu trennen, als das Ereignis des Selbstmordes die zu späten Vorkehrungen rechtfertigte und die Schwierigkeit durchhieb.

Gewiß für jeden, der nicht den ganzen Geist der Worte auf ihren Buchstaben beschränkt, war dieser Selbstmord ein Meuchelmord, verübt von dem Gatten; aber er war auch das Resultat eines außerordentlichen Schwindels der Eifersucht. *Der Eifersüchtige ist vor allem Privateigentümer.* Ich verhinderte den Kreolen, einen unnützen und gefährlichen Skandal zu machen, gefährlich vor allem für das Andenken seiner Geliebten, denn das müßige Publikum hätte das Opfer einer ehebrecherischen Verbindung mit dem Bruder ihres Gatten angeklagt. Ich war Zeuge des Begräbnisses. Niemand außer dem Bruder und mir wußte die Wahrheit. Um mich hörte ich Unwürdigkeiten murmeln über diesen Selbstmord und ich verachtete sie. Man errötet vor der öffentlichen Meinung, wenn man sie in der Nähe sieht mit ihrer feigen Erbitterung und ihren schmutzigen Vermutungen. Die Meinung ist zu gespalten durch die Isolierung der Menschen, zu unwissend, zu verdorben, weil jeder sich selbst und alle sich wechselseitig fremd sind.—

Wenige Wochen verstrichen übrigens, ohne mir Enthüllungen derselben Art zu bringen. In demselben Jahre registrierte ich Liebesverbindungen, verursacht durch Weigerung der Eltern, ihre Zustimmung zu geben, und beendigt mit einem doppelten Pistolenschuß.

Ich notierte ebenso Selbstmorde von Weltmännern, reduziert auf die Impotenz in der Blüte des Alters, die der Mißbrauch des Genusses in eine unüberwindliche Melancholie gestürzt hatte.

Viele Leute endigen ihre Tage unter der Herrschaft des Gedankens, daß die Medizin, nach langer unnützer Quälerei durch ruinierende Vorschriften, unfähig ist, sie von ihren Übeln zu befreien.

Man würde eine seltsame Sammlung von Zitaten berühmter Autoren und Poesien veranstalten können, welche die Verzweifelten schreiben, die mit einem gewissen Prunk ihren Tod vorbereiteten. Während des Augenblicks wundersamer Kaltblütigkeit, welcher dem Entschluß zu sterben folgt, atmet sich eine Art ansteckender Begeisterung aus diesen Seelen aus und strömt auf das Papier, selbst im Schoß der Klassen, die aller Erziehung beraubt sind. Indem sie sich sammeln vor dem Opfer, dessen Tiefe sie durchdenken, faßt sich alle ihre Macht zusammen, um in einem warmen und charakteristischen Ausdrucke zu verbluten.

Einige dieser Gedichte, welche in den Archiven vergraben sind, sind Meisterwerke. Ein schwerfälliger Bourgeois, der seine Seele in sein Geschäft und seinen Gott in den Handel legt, kann alles dies sehr romantisch finden und durch sein Hohnlächeln Schmerzen widerlegen, die er nicht versteht: seine Geringschätzung nimmt uns nicht Wunder. Was anders erwarten von Dreiprozentischen, die nicht einmal ahnen, daß sie täglich and stündlich, Stück vor Stück, sich selbst, ihre menschliche Natur morden! Aber was soll man sagen von den guten Leuten, welche die Devoten, die Gebildeten spielen und welche seine Unflätigkeiten wiederholen? Ohne Zweifel, es ist von einer hohen Wichtigkeit, daß die armen Teufel das Leben ertragen, wäre es auch nur im Interesse der privilegierten Klassen dieser Welt, welche der allgemeine Selbstmord der Kanaille ruinieren würde, aber gäbe es kein anderes Mittel, die Existenz dieser Klasse erträglich zu machen, als die Beleidigung, das Hohnlächeln und die schönen Worte? Überdem muß eine gewisse Art von Seelengröße in dieser Art von Bettlern existieren, welche, entschlossen zum Tode wie sie sind, sich selbst vernichten und nicht den Weg des Selbstmordes durch den Umgang des Schaffots machen. Es ist wahr, daß je weiter unsere Handelsepoche vorschreitet, um so seltner diese edlen Selbstmorde des Elendes werden, und die bewußte Feindseligkeit tritt an die Stelle, und der Elende läuft rücksichtslos die Chancen des Diebstahls und des Meuchelmordes. Man erhält leichter die Todesstrafe als Arbeit.

Ich habe im Durchwühlen der Archive der Polizei nur
ein einziges offenbares Symptom von Feigheit auf der Liste
der Selbstmorde. Es handelte sich um einen jungen
Amerikaner, Wilfrid Ramsay, der sich tötete, um sich nicht
duellieren zu müssen.

Die Klassifikation der verschiedenen Ursachen des Selbstmordes würde die Klassifikation der *Gebrechen selbst
unserer Gesellschaft sein.* Man hat sich getötet, weil man
von Intriganten einer Erfindung beraubt wurde, bei deren
Gelegenheit der Erfinder, gestürzt in das scheußlichste
Elend infolge der langen gelehrten Untersuchungen, denen
er sich hatte hingeben müssen, nicht einmal ein Brevet
kaufen konnte. Man hat sich getötet, um die enormen Kosten
zu vermeiden und die erniedrigende Verfolgung in Geldver-
legenheiten, die übrigens so häufig sind, daß die Männer,
beauftragt mit der Leitung der allgemeinen Interessen, sich
nicht im mindesten darum bekümmern. Man hat sich
getötet, weil man sich keine Arbeit verschaffenn konnte,
nachdem man lange Zeit geseufzt hatte unter den Beleidigungen und dem Geiz derer, die in unserer Mitte die
willkürlichen Distributoren der Arbeit sind.

Ein Arzt konsultierte mich eines Tages über einen Tod,
dessen Veranlassung gewesen zu sein er sich selbst anklagte.

Eines Abends, bei seiner Rückkehr nach Belleville, wo er
wohnte, wurde er in einer kleinen Straße, in deren Hinter-
grund seine Türe war, im Dunkel von einem verschleierten
Weibe angehalten. Sie bat ihn mit zitternder Stimme, sie zu
hören. In einiger Entfernung ging eine Person, deren Gesichts-
züge er nicht unterscheiden konnte, auf und ab spazieren. Sie
wurde überwacht von einem Mann. „Mein Herr," sagte sie
ihm, „ich bin schwanger, und wenn dies entdeckt wird, bin
ich entehrt. Meine Familie, die Meinung der Welt, die Leute
von Ehre werden mir nicht verzeihen. Die Frau, deren Ver-
trauen ich getäuscht habe, würde verrückt und würde sich
unfehlbar von ihrem Manne scheiden lassen. Ich verteidige

nicht meine Sache. Ich stehe mitten in einem Skandal, dessen
Ausbruch mein Tod allein verhindern könnte. Ich wollte
mich töten, man will, daß ich lebe. Man hat mir gesagt, daß
Ihr mitleidig seid, und dies gab mir die Überzeugung, daß Ihr
nicht der Mitschuldige am Mord eines Kindes sein werdet,
wenn auch dies Kind noch nicht in der Welt ist. Ihr seht, es
handelt sich um ein Abtreiben der Frucht. Ich werde mich
nicht zur Bitte erniedrigen, zur Beschönigung dessen, was mir
das verwerflichste Verbrechen scheint. Ich habe nur fremden
Bitten nachgegeben, indem ich mich Euch präsentiere; denn
ich werde zu sterben wissen. Ich rufe den Tod herbei, und
dafür habe ich niemand nötig. Man gibt sich den Anschein,
Vergnügen am Begießen des Gartens zu finden: man zieht
sich dazu Holzschuhe an: man wählt eine schlüpfrige Stelle,
wo man alle Tage Wasser schöpfen geht, man richtet es so ein,
im Behälter der Quelle zu verschwinden; und die Leute sagen,
daß das ein „Unglück" war. Ich habe alles vorhergesehen,
mein Herr. Ich wollte, daß es den andern Morgen wäre, ich
würde von ganzem Herzen gehn. Alles ist vorbereitet, damit
es so sei. Man hat mir gesagt, es Euch zu sagen, ich sage es
Euch. Ihr habt zu entscheiden, ob ein Mord oder ob ihrer zwei
stattfinden werden. Weil man von meiner Feigheit den Eid-
schwur erhalten hat, daß ich mich ohne Rückhalt eurer
Entscheidung überlassen werde.—Entscheidet!"

„Diese Alternative," fuhr der Doktor fort, „entsetzte
mich. Die Stimme dieses Weibes hatte einen reinen und
harmonischen Klang; ihre Hand, die ich in der meinen
hielt, war fein und zart, ihre freie und entschlossene
Verzweiflung verkündigte einen ausgezeichneten Geist.
Aber es handelte sich um einen Punkt, wobei ich mich
wirklich erzittern fühlte, obgleich in tausend Fällen, bei
schwierigen Entbindungen z.B., wenn die chirurgische
Frage zwischen der Rettung der Mutter und der des Kindes
schwebt, die Politik oder die Menschlichkeit ohne Skrupel
nach ihrem Belieben entscheidet."

„Flieht ins Ausland, sagte ich. Unmöglich, erwiderte sie; es ist nicht daran zu denken."

„Ergreift geschickte Vorsichtsmaßregeln!"

„Ich kann sie nicht ergreifen; ich schlafe in demselben Alkoven, wie die Frau, deren Freundschaft ich verraten habe." „Sie ist eure Verwandte?" „Ich darf Euch nicht mehr antworten!"

„Ich hätte," fuhr der Arzt fort, „mein bestes Lebensblut dafür gegeben, dieses Weib vor dem Selbstmord oder dem Verbrechen zu retten, oder, daß sie diesem Konflikt entrinnen könne, ohne meiner zu bedürfen. Ich klagte mich der Barbarei an, weil ich vor der Mitschuld an einem Morde zurückschauderte. Der Kampf war fürchterlich. Dann flüsterte mir ein Dämon ein, daß man sich noch nicht töte, weil man gern sterben wolle; daß man die kompromittierten Leute, indem man ihnen die Macht nehme, Böses zu tun, zwinge, ihren Lastern zu entsagen. Ich erriet Luxus in den Stickereien, die unter ihren Fingern spielten, und die Hülfsquellen des Vermögens aus der eleganten Diktion ihrer Rede. Man glaubt den Reichen weniger Mitleid schuldig zu sein; mein Selbstgefühl empörte sich gegen den Gedanken einer mit Gold aufgewogenen Verführung, obgleich man dies Kapitel bisher nicht berührt hatte, was eine Delikatesse mehr war, und der Beweis, daß man meinen Charakter achtete. Ich gab eine abschlägige Antwort; die Dame entfernte sich schnell; das Geräusch eines Kabriolets überzeugte mich, daß ich nicht wieder gut machen konnte, was ich getan hatte."

„Fünfzehn Tage nachher brachten mir die Zeitungen die Lösung des Geheimnisses. Die junge Nichte eines Pariser Bankiers, höchstens 18 Jahre alt, geliebte Mündel ihrer Tante, die sie nicht mehr aus den Augen gelassen hatte seit dem Tode ihrer Mutter, was ausgeglitscht in einen Bach auf dem Gut ihrer Vormünder, zu Villemomble, und ertrunken. Ihr Vormund war untröstlich; in seiner Eigenschaft als

Onkel durfte er, der feige Verführer, sich seinem Schmerz vor der Welt überlassen." Man sieht, in Ermangelung eines Besseren ist der Selbstmord die äußerste Zuflucht gegen die Übel des Privatlebens. Unter den Ursachen des Selbstmordes habe ich sehr häufig die Entsetzung von Ämtern gezählt, die Verweigerung von Arbeit, den plötzlichen Fall der Saläre, infolgedessen die Familien nicht mehr den notwendigen Lebensunterhalt sich verschaffen konnten, um so mehr, da die Mehrzahl von ihnen aus der Hand in den Mund lebt.

Zur Epoche, wo man im Hause des Königs die Garden reduzierte, wurde ein braver Mann entfernt, wie der ganze Rest und ohne mehr Umstände. Sein Alter und sein Mangel an Protektion erlaubten ihm nicht, sich in die Armee zurückversetzen zu lassen; die Industrie war seiner Unwissenheit verschlossen. Er suchte in die Ziviladministration einzutreten; die Konkurrenten, zahlreich hier wie überall, versperrten ihm diesen Weg. Er verfiel in einen dumpfen Kummer und tötete sich. Man fand in seiner Tasche einen Brief und Aufschlüsse über seine Verhältnisse. Seine Frau war eine arme Nähterin; ihre beiden Töchter, von 16 und 18 Jahren, arbeiteten mit ihr. Tarnau, unser Selbstmörder, sagte in seinen hinterlassenen Papieren, ,,daß, da er seiner Familie nicht mehr nützlich sein könne und da er gezwungen sei, seiner Frau und seinen Kindern zur Last zu leben, er es für seine Pflicht gehalten habe, sich das Leben zu rauben, um sie von diesem Zuwachs an Bürde zu erleichtern; er empfehle seine Kinder der Herzogin von Angoulême; er hoffe von der Güte dieser Prinzessin, daß man Mitleid mit so viel Elend haben werde." Ich verfaßte einen Bericht an den Polizeipräfekten Anglès und nach dem nötigen Geschäftsgang ließ die Herzogin 600 Francs der unglücklichen Familie Tarnau zustellen.

Traurige Hülfe ohne Zweifel, nach einem solchen Verlust! Aber wie sollte eine Familie allen Unglücklichen abhelfen, da, alles berechnet, ganz Frankreich, wie es gegenwärtig ist, sie nicht nähren könnte. Die Wohltätigkeit der Reichen würde hierzu nicht ausreichen, wenn selbst unsere ganze Nation religiös wäre, woven sie weit entfernt ist. *Der Selbstmord hebt den gewaltsamsten Teil der Schwierigkeit auf, das Schaffot den Rest. Nur von einer Umschmelzung unseres allgemeinen Systems der Agrikultur und der Industrie kann man Einkommenquellen und wirklichen Reichtum erwarten.* Auf dem Pergament kann man leicht Konstitutionen proklamieren, das Recht jedes Bürgers auf Erziehung, auf Arbeit und vor allem auf ein Minimum von Subsistenzmitteln. Aber es ist nicht alles damit getan, diese großmütigen Wünsche auf das Papier zu schreiben, es bleibt die eigentliche Aufgabe, diese liberalen Ideen zu befruchten durch materielle und intelligente, durch soziale Institutionen.

Die antike Welt, das Heidentum hat herrliche Schöpfungen auf die Erde geworfen; die moderne Freiheit, wird sie unter ihrer Rivalin zurückbleiben? Wer wird zusammenlöten diese beiden großartigen Elemente der Macht? — So weit Peuchet.

Wir wollen schließlich noch eine von seinen Tabellen über die jährlichen Selbstmorde in Paris geben.

Es geht aus einer andern von Peuchet mitgeteilten Tabelle hervor, daß von 1817–1824 (einbergriffen) 2808 Selbstmorde in Paris stattfanden. Die Zahl ist natürlich in der Wirklichkeit größer. Namentlich von den Ertrunkenen, deren Leichname auf der Morgue ausgestellt werden, weiß man nur in sehr seltenen Fällen, ob sie Selbstmörder waren oder nicht.

Tabelle über die Selbstmorde in Paris während des Jahres 1824

Zahl	1. Semester ....198 2. Semester 173	also 371

Wovon den Versuch des Selbstmords
    überlebt 125
    nicht überlebt 246
Männlichen Geschlechts 239
Weiblichern   " 132
Unverheiratete 207
Verheiratete..164

Todesart
    Schwerer freiwilliger Sturz........................... 47
    Erdroßlung.. 38
    Durch Schneideinstrumente 40
    "   Feuerwaffen... 42
    "   Vergiftungen 28
    "   Kohlenerstickungen 61
    Erstickung durch freiwilligen Sturz
    ins Wasser 115

Motive
    Liebesleidenschaft, häuslicher
    Zank und Kummer 71
    Krankheiten, Lebensüberdruß,
    Geistesschwäche.....................................128
    Schlechte Aufführung, Spiel, Lotterie
    Furcht vor Vorwürfen und Strafen............... 53
    Elend, Not, Verlust von Stellen,
    Arbeitseinstellung.................................... 59
    Unbekannte Motive 60

Du suicide et de ses causes

Jacques Peuchet

Le chiffre annuel des suicides, en quelque façon normal et périodique parmi nous, ne peut être considéré que comme le symptôme d'un vice constitatif de la société moderne, car à l'époque des disettes et dans les hivers rigoureux, ce symptôme est toujours plus manifeste, de même qu'il prend un caractère épidémique lors des haltes de l'industrie et quand les banqueroutes se suc-cèdent en ricochet. La prostitution et le vol grandissent alors dans la même proportion. En principe, bien que la plus large source du suicide découle principalement de la misère, nous le retrouvons dans toutes les classes, chez les riches dé-sœuvrés, comme chez les artistes et les hommes politiques. La diversité des causes qui le motivent nous paraît échapper au blâme uniforme et sans charité des moralistes.

Des maladies de consumption, contre lesquelles la science actuelle est inerte et insuffisante, des amitiés méconnues, des amours trompés, des ambitions qui se découragent, des douleurs de famille, une émulation étouffée, le dégoût d'une vie monotone, un enthousiasme refoulé sur lui-même, sont très certainement des occasions de suicide

[We have not modernized the spellings found in the 1838 original. —EDS.]

pour les natures d'une certaine richesse, et l'amour même de la vie, ressort énergique de la personnalité, conduit fort souvent à se débarrasser d'une existence détestable.

Madame de Staël, qui ressassa beaucoup de lieux communs et les réhabilita quelque temps dans le plus beau style du monde, s'est attachée à démontrer que le suicide est une action contre nature, et que l'on ne saurait le regarder comme un acte de courage; elle a surtout établi qu'il était plus digne de lutter contre le désespoir que d'y succomber. De semblables raisons affectent peu les âmes que le malheur accable. Sont-elles religieuses, elles spéculent sur un meilleur monde; ne croient-elles en rien au contraire, elles cherchent le repos du néant. Les tirades philosophiques n'ont aucune valeur à leurs yeux, et sont d'un faible recours dans le chagrin. Il est surtout absurde de prétendre qu'un acte qui se consomme si fréquemment soit un acte contre nature; le suicide n'est d'aucune manière contre nature, puisque nous en sommes journellement les témoins. Ce qui est contre nature n'arrive pas. Il est au contraire de la nature de notre société d'enfanter beaucoup de suicides; tandis que les Berbères et les Tartares ne se suicident pas. Toutes les sociétés n'ont donc pas les mêmes produits; voilà ce qu'il faut se dire pour travailler à la réforme de la nôtre, et la faire gravir un des échelons supérieurs de la destinée du genre humain. Quant au courage, si l'on passe pour en avoir dès que l'on brave la mort en plein jour et sur le champ de bataille, sous l'empire de toutes les excitations réunies, rien ne prouve que l'on en manque nécessairement quand on se donne la mort soi-même et dans les ténèbres. On ne tranche pas une pareille controverse par des insultes contre les morts. Que le motif qui détermine l'individu à se tuer soit léger ou ne le soit pas, la sensibilité ne saurait se mesurer chez les hommes sur la même échelle; on ne peut pas plus conclure à l'égalité des sensations qu'à celle des caractères et des tempéramens; et tel événement n'excite qu'un sentiment imperceptible chez les uns, qui fait naître une douleur violente chez les autres. Le bonheur ou le malheur ont autant de manières d'être et de se manifester qu'il y a de différences entre les individus et les esprits. Un poète a dit:

Ce qui fait ton bonheur devilendrait mon tourment;
Le prix de ta vertu serait mon châtiment.

Tout ce que l'on a dit contre le suicide tourne dans le même cercle d'idées. On oppose au suicide les décrets de la Providence, sans nous faire lire ces décrets d'une façon bien claire, puisque, après tout, ceux qui se frappent en doutent. Ce peut être par la faute de ceux qui n'auront pas rendu les termes de ces décrets-là intelligibles et satisfaisans. Le diamant de l'Evangile est lui-même resté dans son argile. On nous parle de nos devoirs envers la société, sans que nos droits sur la société soient à leur tour nettement définis et établis; et l'on exalte enfin le mérite plus grand mille fois, dit-on, de surmonter la douleur que d'y succomber, ce qui est un aussi triste mérite qu'une triste perspective. Bref, on en fait un acte de lâcheté, un crime contre les lois et l'honneur.

D'où vient que, malgré tant d'anathèmes, l'homme se tue? C'est que le sang ne coule pas de la même façon dans les veines des gens désespérés que le sang des êtres froids qui se donnent le loisir de débiter tous ces stériles raisonnements.

Peut-être n'a-t-on pas encore étudié toutes les causes qui président au suicide; on n'examine pas assez les subversions de l'âme dans ces terribles momens, et quels germes vénéneux de très longues douleurs ont pu développer insensiblement dans le caractère. L'homme semble un mystère pour l'homme; on ne sait que blâmer et l'on ignore.

A voir combien les institutions sous l'empire desquelles vit l'Europe disposent légèrement du sang et de la vie des peuples, et, aussi, comme la justice civilisée s'environne d'un riche matériel de prisons, de châtimens, d'instrumens de supplice pour la sanction de ses arrêts incertains; et le nombre inoui de classes laissées de toutes parts dans la misère; et les parias sociaux qu'on frappe d'un mépris brutal et préventif pour se dispenser peut-être de les arracher à leur fange; à voir tout cela, on ne conçoit guère en vertu de quel titre on pourrait ordonner à l'individu de respecter sur lui-même une existence dont nos coutumes, nos préjugés, nos lois et nos mœurs font si généralement bon marché.

Quel que soit le motif principal et déterminant du suicide, il est certain que son action agit avec une puissance absolue sur sa volonté. Pourquoi donc s'étonner si, jusqu'à présent, tout ce qu'on a dit ou fait pour vaincre cet entraînement aveugle, est resté sans effet, et si les législateurs et les moralistes ont également échoué dans leurs tentatives? Pour en arriver à comprendre le cœur humain, il faut d'abord avoir la miséricorde et la pitié du Christ.

On a cru pouvoir arrêter les suicides par des peines flétrissantes et par une sorte d'infamie jetée sur la mémoire du coupable. Que dire de l'indignité d'une flétrissure lancée sur des gens qui ne sont plus là pour plaider leur cause? Les malheureux s'en soucient peu du reste; et si le suicide accuse quelqu'un vis-à-vis de Dieu, l'accusation plane surtout sur les gens qui restent, puisque, dans cette foule, pas un n'a mérité que l'on vécût pour lui. Les moyens puérils et atroces qu'on a imaginés ont-ils lutté victorieusement contre les suggestions du désespoir? Qu'importent à l'être qui veut fuir le monde les injures que le monde promet à son cadavre! Il ne voit dans l'ignominie de la claie que l'opinion lui prépare qu'une lâcheté de plus de la part des vivans. Qu'est-ce, en effet, qu'une société où l'on trouve la solitude la plus profonde au sein de plusieurs millions d'âme; où l'on peut être pris d'un désir implacable de se tuer sans que qui que ce soit nous devine? Cette société-là n'est pas une société; c'est, comme le dit Jean-Jacques, un désert peuplé de bêtes féroces.

Dans les places que j'ai remplies à l'administration de la

police, les suites des *suicides* étaient en partie dans mes attributions; j'ai voulu connaître si dans leurs causes déterminantes il ne s'en trouverait pas dont on pût modérer ou prévenir l'effet. J'avais entrepris sur ce sujet important un travail considérable. Sans m'appesantir sur des théories, j'essaierai de présenter des faits.

Parmi les causes de désespoir qui font rechercher la mort aux personnes douées d'une grande susceptibilité nerveuse, aux êtres passionnés et mélancoliques, j'ai remarqué, comme fait prédominant, les mauvais traitemens, les injustices, les peines secrètes, que des parens durs et prévenus, des supérieurs irrités et menaçans, font éprouver aux personnes qui sont dans leur dépendance. La révolution n'a pas fait tomber toutes les tyrannies; les inconvéniens reprochés aux pouvoirs arbitraires subsistent dans les familles; ils y causent des crises analogues à celles des révolutions. Est-il sûr, comme on le suppose, que la crainte de voir leurs amis, leurs parens ou leurs domestiques, livrés à l'infamie, et les corps traînés dans la boue, ramènerait ces hommes impitoyables à la prudence, à la modération, à la justice envers leurs inférieurs, et les porterait à prévenir ainsi des meurtres volontaires, commis dans la pensée de se soustraire à leur domination? Je ne le pense pas; ce serait, par un double sacrilége, souiller deux cultes à la fois, le culte des vivans et le culte des morts. On ne voit pas jusqu'ici que ce moyen ait atteint le but; on y a sagement renoncé.

Pour obtenir un bon résultat sur l'esprit des supérieurs envers leurs subordonnés, et principalement sur les parens entre eux, on a pensé que la crainte de se voir atteint par la diffamation et le scandale public serait encore une mesure efficace. Cette mesure ne suffirait pas, et le blâme plein d'amertume qu'on verse à loisir sur le malheureux qui s'est arraché la vie, diminue chez les provocateurs, si même il n'en éteint le sentiment en eux, la honte de tous ces scandales et la conscience d'en avoir été les vrais provocateurs.

Le clergé me semble plus irreligieux que la société même lorsqu'il donne la main à de si lâches préjugés par le refus de toute sépulture religieuse.

En somme, les rapports entre les intérêts et les esprits, les véritables relations entre les individus, sont à créer de fond en comble parmi nous; et le suicide n'est qu'un des mille et un symptômes de cette lutte sociale, toujours flagrante, dont tant de combattans se retirent parce qu'ils sont las de compter parmi les victimes et parce qu'ils se révoltent contre la pensée de prendre un grade au milieu des bourreaux. En veut-on quelques exemples; je vais les extraire des procès-verbaux authentiques.

Dans le mois de juillet 1816, la fille d'un tailleur, domicilié sous les piliers des halles, était promise en mariage à un étalier boucher, jeune homme de bonnes mœurs, économe et laborieux, très épris de sa jolie fiancée, qui le lui rendait bien. La jeune fille était couturière; elle avait l'estime de tous ceux qui la connaissaient; et les parens de son futur l'aimaient tendrement. Ces braves gens ne laissaient échapper aucune occasion d'anticiper sur la possession de leur bru; on imaginait des parties de plaisir dont elle était la reine et l'idole. L'estime générale ajoutait à l'estime que les fiancés avaient l'un pour l'autre.

L'époque du mariage arrive; tous les arrangemens sont faits entre les deux familles, et les conventions arrêtées. La veille du jour fixé pour se rendre à la municipalité, la jeune fille et ses parens devaient souper dans la famille du jeune homme; un léger incident survint. De l'ouvrage à rendre pour une riche maison de leur clientelle retint au logis le tailleur et sa femme; ils s'excusèrent; mais la mère de l'étalier s'obstinant, vint chercher sa petite bru qui reçut l'autorisation de la suivre.

Malgré l'absence de deux des principaux convives, le repas fut des plus joyeux. Il se débita beaucoup de ces gaudrioles de famille que la perspective d'une noce autorise. La

belle-mère se voyait déjà marraine d'un gros poupon. On
but, on chanta. L'avenir fut mis sur le tapis. Fort avant dans
la nuit, on se trouvait encore à table. Par une tolérance qui
s'explique, les parens du jeune homme, enthousiasmés de
leurs enfans et jouissant de leur double tendresse, fermèrent les yeux sur le tacite accord des deux futurs. Les
mains se cherchaient; le feu se mettait aux poudres.
L'amour et la familiarité leur montaient la tête. Après tout,
l'on regardait le mariage comme fait; et ces pauvres jeunes
gens se fréquentaient depuis long-temps sans que l'on eût le
plus léger reproche à leur adresser! Jamais les plaisirs d'un
bon mariage n'avaient été analysés plus vivement. L'atten-
drissement du père et de la mère du fiancé, à qui ce couple
d'amoureux rappelait des souvenirs de jeunesse, l'heure
avancée, des désirs mutuels et déprisonnés par la tolérance
de leurs mentors, la gaieté sans gêne qui règne toujours
dans de semblables repas, tout cela réuni, et l'occasion qui
s'offrait en souriant, et le vin qui pétillait dans les cerveaux,
tout favorisait un dénoûment qui se devine. Les amoureux
se retrouvèrent dans l'ombre, lorsque l'on eut éteint les
lumières. On fit semblant de n'y rien comprendre, de ne pas
s'en douter. Leur bonheur n'avait là que des amis et pas
d'envieux. Le fond prit un instant le pas sur la forme, et ce
plaisir à demi dérobé ne dut en être que plus doux.

La jeune fille ne retourna chez ses parens que le lendemain
matin. Ce qui prouve combien elle se croyait peu coupable,
c'est qu'elle y revint seule. Son tort était grand sans doute,
n'eût-elle considéré que l'inquiétude des siens grâce au pro-
longement d'absence; mais si jamais la bonté, l'indulgence, la
prudence, la retenue, furent imposées à des parens envers un
enfant, ce devait être dans une circonstance pareille, puisque
tout s'apprêtait pour légitimer l'escapade amoureuse. De plus
coupables ont été plus heureux.

La petite se glissa dans sa chambre et dépêcha sa toilette;
mais ses parens l'eurent à peine aperçue, que, dans un accès

de colère dont on ne put les détourner, ils prodiguèrent à leur fille, avec acharnement, tous les noms, toutes les épithètes dont on peut se servir pour vouer l'imprudence au déshonneur. Le voisinage en fut témoin, le scandale n'eut pas de bornes. Jugez de la secousse dans une âme qui se sentait vierge par sa pudeur et par le mystère que l'on outrageait. Vainement l'enfant éperdue représentait à ses parens qu'ils la livraient eux-mêmes à la diffamation, qu'elle avouait son tort, sa folie, sa désobéissance; mais que tout allait être réparé. Ses raisons et sa douleur ne désarmèrent pas leur furie. Compères et commères accoururent à l'éclat, et firent chorus. Le sentiment de la honte qui résultait de cette scène affreuse fit prendre à l'enfant la résolution de s'ôter la vie; elle descendit, d'un pas rapide, à travers les malédictions, et courut, l'égarement dans les yeux, se précipiter à la rivière; les mariniers ne la retirèrent de l'eau que morte, et parée de ses ornemens de noces. Comme de raison, ceux qui s'étaient d'abord mis contre la fille, se tournèrent aussitôt contre les parens: cette catastrophe épouvantait leurs âmes.

Peu de jours après, les parens vinrent réclamer à la police une chaîne d'or, que l'enfant portait à son cou, et que le père de son futur lui avait donnée, une montre d'argent doré, des boucles d'oreilles et une bague garnie d'une petite émeraude, tous objets qui avaient été déposés dans les bureaux, comme on le pense bien.

Je ne manquai pas de reprocher avec force à ces gens leur imprudence et leur barbarie. Dire à ces forcenés qu'ils en rendraient compte devant Dieu, vu leurs préjugés étroits, et le manque de religion qui règne dans les basses classes mercantiles, c'aurait été leur faire trop peu d'impression; la cupidité les attirait, plus que le désir de posséder deux ou trois reliques; je crus pouvoir les punir par là. Ils réclamaient les bijoux de la jeune fille; je les leur refusai; je gardai les certificats dont ils avaient besoin pour retirer ces effets de la caisse où, suivant l'usage, on les avait déposés. Tant que je fus à ce poste, ils eurent tort dans leurs réclamations, et je pris plaisir à braver leurs injures. Ce n'est que depuis ma sortie qu'ils en ont obtenu la remise.

La même année, un jeune créole, d'une figure charmante, appartenant à l'une des plus riches familles de la Martinque, se présenta dans mon bureau, et, dès que nous fûmes seuls, me fit la révélation d'une de ces plaies qui laissent d'incurables ulcères au foyer de la vie privée. Il venait s'opposer formellement à la remise du cadavre d'une jeune femme, sa belle-sœur, que le mari, propre frère du créole, réclamait depuis la veille. Cette femme s'était noyée. Ce genre de mort volontaire est le plus fréquent. Les préposés à la fouille de la rivière avaient retrouvé le corps non loin de la grève d'Argenteuil. Par un de ces instincts réfléchis de pudeur qui domine les femmes, jusque dans l'aveuglement du désespoir, la triste victime avait noué soigneusement la frange de sa robe autour de ses pieds. Cette précaution pudique prouvait le suicide jusqu'à l'évidence. A peine était-elle défigurée lorsque les mariniers la transportèrent à la Morgue. Sa beauté, sa jeunesse, la richesse de ses vêtemens, prêtaient à mille conjectures sur la cause première de cette catastrophe. L'affliction du mari, qui la reconnut le premier, passait d'ailleurs les bornes; il ne comprenait pas le premier mot de ce malheur, du moins me l'avait-on dit; je n'avais pas encore vu cet homme. Je représentai au créole que nul ne pouvait prévaloir contre les droits et la réclamation du mari qui faisait en ce moment élever un magnifique tombeau de marbre pour ensevelir les restes inanimés de sa femme. «Aprés l'avoir tuée, le monstre!» criait le créole en se promenant avec agitation.

A la chaleur du désespoir de ce jeune homme, à ses supplications pour que j'obtempérasse à ses vœux, à ses larmes, je crus reconnaître des symptômes d'amour, et je le lui dis. Il me l'avoua; mais en me jurant, avec les attestations les plus vives, que sa belle-sœur n'en avait jamais rien su. Seulement, pour mettre à l'abri la réputation de sa belle-sœur que ce meurtre volontaire pouvait faire accuser d'une intrigue par l'opinion publique toujours prompte à noircir le chagrin, il prétendait produire à la lumière les barbaries de son frère, fallût-il s'asseoir pour cela lui-même sur la sellette d'un tribunal. Il me suppliait de le guider dans cette affaire. A travers le décousu de sa révélation emportée, voici ce que je recueillis. M. de M...., frère de ce créole, homme à bonnes fortunes, avec des goûts d'artiste aimant le luxe et la vie de représentation, s'était uni depuis moins d'un an à cette jeune femme, sous les auspices d'une inclination réciproque; ils formaient le plus beau couple que l'on pût voir. Après le mariage, un vice de sang, venu de famille peut-être, s'était déclaré tout à coup et violemment dans la constitution du nouvel époux. Cet homme, si fier d'un beau physique, d'une tournure élégante, et d'une perfection de formes qui semblaient ne pas lui permettre de craindre des rivaux autour de lui, travaillé tout à coup par un mal inconnu contre les ravages duquel la science avait échoué, s'était misérablement transformé des pieds à la tête. Il avait perdu ses cheveux; sa colonne vertébrale s'était déviée; de jour en jour, la maigreur et les rides le métamorphosaient à vue d'œil; pour les autres, du moins! car son amour-propre essayait de se soustraire à l'évidence. Mais ceci ne l'alitait pas; une vigueur de fer semblait triompher des atteintes de ce mal; il se survivait vigoureusement dans ses propres débris. Le corps tombait en ruines et l'âme restait debout. Il continuait de donner des fêtes, de présider à des parties de chasse, et de mener le riche et fastueux train de vie qui paraissait la loi de son caractère et de sa nature. Cependant, les avanies, les quolibets, les mots plaisans des écoliers et des gamins lorsqu'il se promenait à cheval dans les promenades, des sourires désobligeans et moqueurs, d'officieux avertissements d'amis sur les nombreux ridicules qu'il se donnait par l'obstination de ses manières galantes auprès des femmes dont il devenait le plastron, dissipèrent enfin son illusion et le mirent sur ses gardes vis-à-vis de lui-même. Dès qu'il s'avoua sa laideur et sa difformité, dès qu'il en eut la conscience, son caractère s'aigrit, des pusillanimités lui vinrent. Il parut moins empressé de conduire sa femme aux soirées, aux bals, aux concerts; il se réfugia dans sa demeure, à la campagne; supprima les invitations, élimina des gens sous mille prétextes; et les politesses de ses amis envers sa femme, tolérées par lui tant que l'orgueil lui donnait la certitude de sa supériorité, le rendirent jaloux, soupçonneux, violent. Il voyait dans tous ceux qui persévéraient à le fréquenter le parti pris de faire capituler le cœur de celle qui lui restait comme son dernier orgueil et sa dernière consolation. Vers ce temps, le créole arriva de la Martinique pour des affaires dont la réinstallation des Bourbons sur le trône de France semblait devoir favoriser la réussite. Sa belle-sœur lui fit un excellent accueil; et, dans le naufrage des relations sans nombre qu'elle avait contractées, mais qu'il fallut voir s'engloutir, le nouveau venu conserva les avantages que son titre de frère lui donnait tout naturellement auprès de M. de M.... Notre créole prévit la solitude qui se formerait autour de ce ménage, tant par les querelles directes que son frère eut avec plusieurs amis, que par mille procédés indirects pour en venir à chasser et à décourager les visiteurs. Sans trop se rendre compte de l'impulsion amoureuse qui le rendait exclusif lui-même, le créole approuva ces idées de retraite, et les favorisa même de ses conseils. M. de M.... taillant dans le vif, finit par se retirer tout-à-fait dans une jolie maison de Passy, qui devint en peu de temps un désert.

La jalousie s'alimente des moindres choses. Quand elle ne sait à quoi se prendre, elle se consume et s'ingénie; tout lui sert d'aliment. Peut-être la jeune femme regrettait-elle les plaisirs de son âge. Des murs interceptèrent la vue des

habitations voisines; les persiennes furent fermées du matin
au soir. M. de M.... rôdait avec des armes pendant la nuit, et
faisait sa ronde avec des chiens. Il s'imaginait apercevoir
des traces sur le sable, et créait des suppositions étranges à
propos d'une échelle changée de place par le jardinier. Le
jardinier lui-même, ivrogne presque sexagénaire, fut mis à
la porte. L'esprit d'exclusion n'a pas de frein dans ses ou-
trages, il va jusqu'à l'imbécilité. Le frère, innocent complice
de tout cela, comprit enfin qu'il travaillait au malheur de la
jeune femme, qui, de jour en jour surveillée, insultée, privée
de tout ce qui pouvait distraire une imagination riche et
heureuse, devint chagrine et mélancolique autant qu'elle
avait été franche et rieuse. Elle pleurait et cachait ses
larmes, mais la trace en était assez visible. Un remords vint
au créole. Résolu de s'expliquer naïvement avec sa belle-
sœur, et de réparer une faute à laquelle un sentiment furtif
d'amour donnait assurément naissance, il se glissa de bon
matin sous un bosquet où de temps en temps la captive
allait prendre l'air et cultiver des fleurs. En usant de cette
liberté si restreinte, elle se savait, il faut le croire, sous l'œil
de son jaloux; car, à l'aspect de son beau-frère, qui se trouvait pour la première fois et à l'improviste en tête-à-tête
avec elle, la jeune femme montra la plus grande alarme. Elle
joignit les mains: —Eloignez-vouz, au nom du ciel! lui dit-
elle avec terreur; éloignez-vous!

Et, de fait, le beau-frère eut à peine le temps de se cacher
dans une serre, que M. de M.... survint. Le créole entendit
des éclats, il voulut écouter; le battement de son cœur l'em-
pêcha de saisir le plus léger mot d'une explication que cette
fuite, si le mari la découvrait, pouvait rendre plus
déplorable encore. Cet incident aiguillonna le beau-frère; il
y vit la nécessité d'être dès ce jour le protecteur d'une victime. Il s'efforça de sacrifier toute arrière-pensée d'amour,
dans la résolution de se dévouer pour sa belle-sœur. L'amour
peut aller jusqu'au renoncement le plus absolu, sans abdi-

quer néanmoins son droit de protectorat, car ce dernier renoncement serait d'un lâche. Il continua de voir son frère, prêt à lui parler franchement, à s'avouer, à lui dire tout. M. de M.... n'avait pas encore de soupçons de ce côté; mais cette persistance de son frère en fit naître. Sans lire trop clairement dans les causes de cet intérêt, M. de M.... s'en méfia, prévoyant ce que l'intérêt pourrait devenir. Le créole comprit bientôt que son frère n'était pas toujours absent, comme il le prétendait après coup, toutes les fois que l'on venait inutilement sonner à la porte de la maison de Passy. Un ouvrier serrurier fit les clefs que l'on voulut sur le modèle de celles que son bourgeois avait déjà forgées pour M. de M.... Le créole ne s'effrayait pas des chiens de garde: les chiens le connaissaient. Après un éloignement de dix jours, rouerie assez habile de l'époux, le créole, exaspéré par la crainte, et se mettant lui-même des chimères dans l'esprit, pénétra de nuit dans l'enclos, franchit une grille placée devant la cour principale, atteignit les toits au moyen d'une échelle, et se glissa le long des plombs jusque sous la fenêtre d'un grenier qui lui permit d'arriver près de la chambre à coucher de son beau-frère. Des exclamations violentes lui donnèrent la facilité d'arriver contre une porte vitrée. Ce qu'il vit le navra. La clarté d'une lampe éclairait l'alcove. Sous les rideaux, les cheveux en désordre et la figure pourpre de rage, M. de M.... à demi-nu, agenouillé près de sa femme et sur le lit même dont elle n'osait sortir, quoiqu'en se dérobant à demi, l'accablait des reproches les plus sanglans, et semblait un tigre prêt à la mettre en pièces.

—Oui! lui disait-il, je suis hideux, je suis un monstre, et je ne le sais que trop; je te fais peur. Tu voudrais qu'on te débarrassât de moi, qu'on te délivrât de ma vue. Tu désires l'instant qui te rendra libre. Et ne me dis pas le contraire; je devine ta pensée dans ton effroi, dans ta répugnance, dans tes larmes. Tu rougis des indignes sourires que j'excite, et je te révolte! Tu comptes sans doute une par une les minutes qui doivent s'écouler jusqu'à ce que je ne t'obsède plus de mes infirmités et de ma présence. Tiens! il me prend des désirs affreux, des rages de te défigurer, de te rendre semblable à moi, pour que tu ne puisses conserver l'espoir de te consoler avec tes amans du malheur de m'avoir connu. Je briserai toutes les glaces de cette maison, pour qu'elles ne me reprochent pas un contraste, pour qu'elles cessent d'alimenter ton orgueil. Ne faudrait-il pas te mener ou te laisser aller dans le monde, pour voir chacun t'encourager à me haïr? Non, non! tu ne sortiras d'ici qu'après m'avoir tué. Tue-moi! Préviens ce que je suis tenté de faire tous les jours. Tue-moi!

Et le forcené se roulait sur le lit avec des cris, avec des grincements, de l'écume aux lèvres et mille symptômes de frénésie, avec des coups qu'il se portait lui-même dans sa fureur, près de cette femme éperdue qui lui prodiguait les caresses les plus tendres et les supplications les plus pathétiques. Enfin elle le dompta. La miséricorde avait sans doute remplacé l'amour; mais ce n'était pas assez pour cet homme devenu si repoussant, et dont les passions avaient encore tant d'énergie. Un long abattement fut la suite de cette scène qui pétrifia le créole. Il frémit, et ne sut à qui s'adresser pour soustraire la malheureuse à ce supplice. Cette scène, évidemment, devait se renouveler tous les jours; car, dans les spasmes qui la suivirent, madame de M.... recourut à des fioles préparées par elle, à dessein de rendre un peu de calme à son bourreau. Le créole, à Paris, représentait à lui seul, pour le moment, la famille de M. de M....; peut-être deviendrait-il dangereux de risquer une démarche. C'est dans ce cas surtout que l'on pourrait maudire la lenteur des formes juridiques et l'insouciance des lois que rien ne ferait sortir de leurs allures compassées, parce qu'après tout, il ne s'agissait que d'une femme, l'être que le législateur entoure le moins de garanties. Une lettre de cachet, une mesure arbitraire auraient seules prévenu des malheurs que le témoin de ces rages prévoyait trop. Il se résolut pourtant à risquer le tout pour le tout, sauf à prendre les suites à son compte, sa fortune le mettant à même de faire d'énormes sacrifices, et de ne pas craindre la responsabilité de toutes les audaces. Déjà des médecins de ses amis, déterminés comme lui-même, préparaient une irruption dans la maison de M. de M.... pour constater ces momens de délire et séparer de vive force les deux époux, lorsque l'événement du suicide, en éclatant, justifia des prévisions tardives et trancha la difficulté.

Certes, pour quiconque ne borne pas tout l'esprit des mots à leur lettre, ce suicide était un assassinat; mais il était aussi le résultat d'un vertige extraordinaire de jalousie; et le malheureux mari, qui survécut fort peu de temps à sa femme, échappait à l'accusation de son frère autant à la faveur des termes exprès de notre législation que par l'exagération même du penchant qui le rendait coupable. On juge bien que cette affaire n'eut pas d'autres suites, et que je parvins, sinon à rendre la paix au créole, du moins à l'empêcher de faire un éclat inutile et dangereux. Dangereux surtout pour la mémoire de celle qu'il aimait, car les désœuvrés auraient accusé la victime d'une liaison adultère avec le frère de son mari. Le cadavre fut remis à M. de M...., dont la douleur occupa la capitale par une scène déchirante au cimetière Montmartre, lorsque le prêtre jeta la dernière pellerée de cendre sur le cercueil. J'en fus témoin, et le reproche expira sur mes lèvres. Personne ne sut, sinon le frère et moi, la vérité de cette triste affaire, et le coupable même, trop amoureux de sa victime pour lire dans son propre cœur, semblait l'ignorer comme tout le monde. J'entendis murmurer autour de moi des ignominies sur ce suicide, et je les méprisai. On rougit de l'opinion publique lorsqu'on la voit de près, avec ses lâches acharnemens et ses sales conjectures.

Peu de semaines au reste s'écoulaient sans m'apporter des révélations de ce genre.

Dans la même année, j'enregistrai des conventions amoureuses, causées par les refus de parens, terminées par un double coup de pistolet.

Je notai pareillement des suicides d'hommes du monde, réduits à l'impuissance à la fleur de l'âge, et que l'abus des plaisirs avait plongés dans une insurmontable mélancolie.

Beaucoup de gens mettent fin à leurs jours sous l'empire de cette obsession que la médecine, après les avoir inutilement tourmentés par des prescriptions ruineuses, est impuissante à les délivrer de leurs maux.

On ferait un curieux recueil, aussi, des citations d'auteurs célèbres et des pièces de vers écrites par les désespérés qui se piquent d'un certain faste dans les préparatifs de leur mort. Pendant le moment d'étrange sang-froid qui succède à la résolution de mourir, une sorte d'inspiration contagieuse s'exhale de ces âmes et déborde sur le papier, même au sein des classes les plus dépourvues d'éducation. En se recueillant devant le sacrifice dont elles sondent la profondeur, toute leur puissance se résume pour s'épancher dans une expression chaude et caractéristique.

Quelques-unes des pièces de vers qui sont enfouies dans les archives sont des chefs-d'œuvre. Un lourd bourgeois qui met son âme dans le trafic et son Dieu dans le commerce, peut trouver tout cela très romanesque, et réfuter par ses ricanemens des douleurs dont il n'a pas l'intelligence: son dédain ne nous étonne pas. Mais que dire des bonnes gens qui font les dévots, et qui répètent ces grossièretés?... Sans doute, il est d'une haute importance que les pauvres diables supportent la vie, ne fût-ce que dans l'intérêt des classes privilégiées de ce monde que le suicide universel de la canaille ruinerait; mais n'y aurait-il pas d'autre moyen de faire supporter l'existence à cette canaille que les avanies, les ricanemens et les belles paroles? D'ailleurs il doit exister quelque noblesse d'âme dans ces sortes de gueux qui, décidés qu'ils sont à la mort, se frappent sans chercher d'autres ressources, et ne prennent pas le chemin du suicide par le détour de l'échafaud. Il est vrai que, dans les époques d'incrédulité, ces suicides généreux de la misère tendent à devenir de plus en plus rares; l'hostilité se dessine, et le misérable court franchement les chances du vol et de l'assassinat. On obtient plus facilement la peine capitale que de l'ouvrage.

Je n'ai remarqué dans la fouille des archives de la police qu'un seul symptôme de lâcheté bien manifeste sur la liste des suicides. Il s'agissait d'un jeune Américain, Wilfrid Ramsay, qui se donna la mort pour ne pas se battre en duel. Il avait été souffleté par un garde-du-corps dans un bal public. Sa justification fut donnée par un quaker dans une feuille du temps que j'avais gardée et que je ne retrouve pas. Son défenseur l'accusait encore, et lui reprochait de ne pas avoir su porter noblement le poids de cet affront.

La classification des diverses causes de suicides serait la classification même des vices de la société. Mon dessein n'est pas de me livrer à cette analyse difficile, que le législateur doit aborder pourtant s'il veut extirper souverainement de notre sol les germes de dissolution où notre génération croît et dépérit comme au sein d'une ivraie qui la ronge. On s'est tué pour la spoliation d'une découverte par des intrigans, à l'occasion de laquelle l'inventeur, plongé dans la plus affreuse détresse par suite des recherches savantes auxquelles il avait dû se livrer, ne pouvait même prendre un brevet. On s'est tué pour éviter les frais énormes et l'humiliation des poursuites dans les embarras pécuniaires, si fréquens, du reste, que les hommes chargés de la régie des intérêts généraux ne s'en inquiètent pas le moins du monde. On s'est tué faute de pouvoir se procurer du travail, après avoir long-temps gémi sous les avanies et l'avarice de ceux qui en sont, au milieu de nous, les distributeurs arbitraires. La législation, providence sociale et secondaire, doit un compte de sang à Dieu, son premier législateur et le nôtre, de tout ce qui avorte dans les misères du corps, dans les souffrances de l'âme, dans les élans de l'esprit. On ne peut pas se trouver quitte envers les vivans par des insultes sur les tombeaux.

Je rentre dans les misères de la vie privée, ma thèse favorite.

Une dame Terson, qui tenait sous l'empire un pensionnat de jeunes demoiselles dans le faubourg du Temple, ruinée par l'effet du bonapartisme extravagant qu'elle se fit un devoir d'afficher après le désastre de Waterloo, ce qui donna des scrupules à tous les parens, parce que l'on rassemblait chez elle des conciliabules, vivait depuis 1816 hors barrières, avec sa fille, dans un état voisin de la misère, quand un capitaine retraité, sachant leurs malheurs, et d'où ces malheurs provenaient, lia connaissance avec les deux solitaires. Il s'éprit même de la jeune fille; et, malgré la disproportion des âges, moitié par sympathie d'opinions, moitié pour offrir au petit ménage des secours que ces deux femmes pussent accepter sans rougir, il parla de se marier; la mère le prit au mot.

Quant à la fille, comme toutes les filles tenues sous la discipline de la famille, elle ne semblait avoir d'autres volontés que celles de sa mère. La déclaration du capitaine fut reçue avec reconnaissance. Deux mois après, mademoiselle Terson devenait madame Dufresne. A la suite de ce mariage, madame Terson, femme d'un caractère absolu, faite pour se déployer dans un vaste cercle d'occupations et non pour se résigner à la monotonie mesquine d'une vie retirée, s'aperçut que l'autorité qu'elle exerçait autrefois sur sa fille déclinait insensiblement; elle ne s'y résigna pas et se mit en tête de reconquérir son pouvoir. Ces trempes de caractère, qui montrent tant de ressorts dans un large horizon, dépensent sur un seul personnage, au risque de l'excéder et lorsqu'ils sont rabattus entre les quatre murailles de la vie domestique, la même verve qu'ils emploieraient si magnifiquement au bénéfice d'un ménage de cinq cents personnes. Elles se font insupportables; elles vous crucifient du matin au soir pour se tenir en haleine. La richesse de leur nature devient un fléau. Des plaintes, la mère en vint aux reproches, des reproches aux allusions piquantes, que sa fille la priait d'expliquer, n'y concevant rien, disait-elle, quoique avec un certain tremblement. Le mari souffrait et ne disait rien. Il entrevoyait le moment pénible où il lui faudrait intervenir et se décider pour une rupture, tant le calme semblait impossible à ramener entre ces natures dont il devinait trop tard l'antipathie. Une très jeune femme n'a jamais tort devant une vieille belle-mère. On devine que le capitaine penchait vers son faible; il ne s'en cachait pas. De jour en jour, de plus en plus, les deux femmes semblaient se braver et préluder par des escarmouches à de plus rudes batailles. M. Dufresne prévoyait un enfer. Tout à coup, comme par enchantement, la paix revint, et, avec la paix, des témoignages de cordialité plus que suspects. La régie du ménage revint par la même occasion tout entière à madame Terson, qui trancha, décida, régna. M. Dufresne en fut intrigué malgré lui. Les jeunes femmes ne sont jamais si résignées à retomber sous la griffe maternelle, à moins qu'elles n'aient de certaines raisons. Quelles pouvaient être ces raisons? Il pressa sa femme de lui donner le mot de cette énigme, ce qu'elle écarta d'abord en riant, puis, et parce qu'il y revint, par des excuses en l'air dont il ne crut pas un mot, tout en y donnant les mains de peur d'irriter sa petite amie.

Ce fut du côté de la mère qu'il dirigea ses questions, en lui rappelant des paroles singulièrement équivoques dont il avait commenté le sens de mille manières. Comme on éludait aussi de ce côté-là, il se tut; mais il observa les moindres symptômes et ne tarda pas à savoir au plus juste que la mère imposait une étrange réserve aux scrupules de sa fille dès que celle-ci se mettait en révolte, rien que par une indication mystérieuse vers une certaine armoire de l'appartement. Prendre prétexte d'une acquisition intéressante à faire, écarter ces deux ennemies en les expédiant sous ce prétexte, faire venir un serrurier et procéder à l'investigation des papiers de la cachette, ce fut la rubrique naturelle du mari; sa curiosité fut malheureusement servie par une découverte cruelle. Madame Dufresne, alors qu'elle n'était encore que mademoiselle Terson, avait eu, dans le même temps, trois fantaisies de cœur avec des jeunes officiers bonapartistes qui venaient flatter les opinions de la mère pour profiter des bonnes volontés de la fille. Malgré la gravité du chiffre, l'âge l'excusera peut-être auprès de ceux qui se disent combien la réserve idiote des mères devient funeste aux filles à l'époque où leur constitution physique s'enrichit tout à coup d'un élément indomptable qui les rend inquiètes et curieuses. Les lettres étaient, du reste, rangées avec les réponses par ordre de date, en liasses parfaitement spéciales et distinctes. Rien de plus audacieux, de plus mêlé, de plus hardi que cette triple intrigue, où chacun des amans avait reçu, dans une brillante variété de style, les assurances d'un amour unique et d'une éternelle fidélité. Les dates, un peu trop rapprochées, faisaient foi d'un triple mensonge à cet égard, et, grâce à l'ingénuité de ces gentillesses épistolaires, on ne pouvait former le plus léger doute. Mais comment les lettres de mademoiselle Terson se trouvaient-elles avec les lettres de ses bons amis?... M. Dufresne eut l'explication de cette réunion bizarre par la mention dans ces lettres du nom d'une ouvrière que mademoiselle Terson chargeait de porter les missives à la poste. Il se souvint de l'aversion décidée que sa femme avait pour cette ouvrière, ainsi que des regards triomphans et des chuchoteries insolentes de madame Terson lorsque cette ouvrière venait la voir. Il en conclut, sans recourir à de plus amples informations, que la confidente avait trahi sa jeune amie par la suggestion de la mère, et, sur cette donnée, se convainquit, en examinant bien, que la confidente avait encore suggéré la correspondance pour en abuser; chaos d'infamies dont les intrigues de mademoiselle Terson étaient encore les plus vénielles.

L'ascendant tout nouveau de madame Terson se trouvait dès lors motivé par quelque explication récente à cet égard. La mère s'était indignement forgé des armes contre sa fille pour la dominer en quelque temps que ce fût. Dieu sait dans quels desseins!... M. Dufresne était un galant homme; quoique de son siècle en beaucoup de points, il n'établissait pas complaisamment deux morales contradictoires, l'une au profit des hommes, sans frein et sans mesure, l'autre au désavantage des femmes, puritaine, retrécie; et, par ses fredaines passées, il avait appris à se montrer tolérant. La fourberie produisait sur lui l'effet qu'elle produit sur les meilleures âmes, qui la conçoivent quand ils comprennent nos mœurs, l'excusent et la justifient au besoin, parce que la fourberie est le droit de l'esclave, et que les femmes sont esclaves. Mais on a beau la concevoir, on en souffre. En vain il essaya de reprendre son train de vie et son air de confiance, le cœur saignait. Il ne put cacher assez habilement sa tristesse, que madame Dufresne ne s'en inquiétât. De plus, à toutes les maximes de rigueur qu'elle se permettait dans l'occasion sur les menées secrètes du tiers et du quart, diplomatie courante des femmes qui pensent travailler à leur propre apologie en se parant d'une inflexible sévérité de principes, le capitaine répondait quelquefois avec un rire plein d'amertume.

Madame Dufresne, éclairée par ces symptômes, se sentit perdue dans l'esprit de son mari. Sa fierté s'en effraya. Lorsque nous ne puisons pas notre force dans nous-mêmes, notre vie est tout entière dans le cœur des autres; s'ils sont ouverts et bons, nous reprenons notre estime et notre courage dans leur intelligence. De fait, elle se sentait irréprochable dans le présent, et ne se devait à son mari qu'à partir du jour de sa libre promesse. La fidélité du passé n'est pas obligatoire. Elle voulut parler, tomber à ses pieds, obtenir un pardon, dire à cet homme les tourmens d'une adolescence de flamme au milieu des premières fièvres d'un tempérament plein d'énergie. Puis elle se révolta contre l'idée de s'humilier ainsi devant l'un de ceux que son sexe se reconnaît le droit de tenir à ses genoux. L'amour, c'est la royauté des femmes, leur élément, leur vie. Toutes répugnent dans le fond du cœur à se croire soumises au jugement de qui que ce soit sur ce point. Quand vous devinez leurs antécédens, vous ne faites que voir clair dans leur nature; mais vous n'avez pas le droit de blâme, parce que, à moins que l'on ne soit un sot, on ne blâme pas un élément qui ne saurait s'empêcher d'être. Dès ce jour, elle souffrit mort et martyre, s'irritant et pleurant tour à tour, devenant sombre et emportée. Les querelles entre elle et sa mère reprirent avec de nouvelles alternatives de réconciliations et de récriminations; si bien, qu'un jour, sous un prétexte en l'air et par un raffinement de cruauté dont une femme seule est capable dans ses vengeances, les trois officiers bonapartistes se trouvèrent invités à une soirée de M. Dufresne. La mère, à la vérité, ne croyait pas ce dernier instruit, et ne voulait que faire ployer sa fille par l'audace et l'éclat de ce coup de théâtre. Elle supposait la délicatesse de chacun de ces jeunes gens, et qu'aucun d'eux ne pensait dans le fond de l'âme avoir été le jouet de sa fille. Le capitaine ne put supporter cette avanie; il se retira, et sa femme l'entendit murmurer tout bas: «C'est trop fort!...» Madame Dufresne s'échappa de son côté, fit porter par un domestique un mot à sa mère, et disparut. On s'étonnait cependant de ne pas voir les maîtres de la maison; leur absence devenait un sujet d'étonnement et de mortification. Ce mot remis devant tout le monde et de la part de la femme qui devait faire les honneurs du cercle, arracha des cris à la mère. Elle comprit, mais trop tard, que son stupide acharnement venait de tout perdre. On courut vainement sur les traces de l'infortunée; nul ne put donner de ses nouvelles. M. Dufresne manifesta, mais inutilement, son indulgence: le coup venait d'être porté. On retrouva le lendemain matin le corps de madame Dufresne horriblement mutilé sur un des bateaux de charbon qui stationnent contre les arches du pont Marie.

C'est presque toujours avec un ton railleur d'incrédulité que l'on repousse les pronostics indiscrets sortis de la bouche du désespoir. On les taxe d'abord de banalités vaines; le suicide devant être, suivant l'opinion assez leste de ceux qui ne veulent pas qu'on les en occupe, du nombre de ces choses que l'on fait et dont on ne se vante point. En général, l'expression du malheur des autres nous importune. A celui qui se plaint de ses douleurs, on répond: — Croyez-vous donc que nous n'avons pas les nôtres?... Et l'on s'imagine avoir mis un baume suffisant sur sa plaie. On se dispense du reste.

S'il est juste de dire que tous les gens qui ont parlé de se mettre à mort se sont pour la plupart résignés à vivre, toujours est-il que ce symptôme n'a jamais fait défaut au chagrin de ceux qui prirent une détermination plus en rapport avec leurs paroles. Ainsi, nourrissez dans l'âme un chagrin secret, on ne vous devinera pas; mais que le secret vous en échappe, on sourira de ce que vous aurez dit. Voilà votre alternative. Cherchez ou ne cherchez pas de recours, c'est tout comme.

Le désespoir se trouve donc parmi nous repoussé de la cécité à l'incrédulité, double résultat de l'isolement des familles et de l'insouciance inévitable des mœurs; et c'est entre ces deux écueils que l'on se tue. Il va bien à la société de déblatérer après cela sur ses victimes!...

Marianne Flidorf, jeune brodeuse, qui paraissait avoir des

dispositions pour les lettres, avait épousé en 1814 un nommé Charles Guinchy, modeste employé d'une administration publique, que ses chefs aimaient et devaient lancer. Ce mariage était le résultat d'un coup de tête, après le conseil d'une amie, fine mouche qui, politiquement, avait fait comprendre à Marianne qu'elle ne pourrait se produire à sa guise dans le monde que sous le chaperon d'un mari. Ce conseil, colporté de droite à gauche, transpira quelque temps avant la noce, et Charles s'en alarma de peur de pis. La brodeuse, résolue d'en venir à ses fins, le guérit pour le moment de ses scrupules par un argument qui lui ferma la bouche, et que les jeunes femmes ont toujours à leur service dans les cas désespérés.

L'employé, convaincu dès lors que Marianne lui ferait tous les sacrifices, et que l'esprit même de considération le cédait à l'amour qu'on avait pour lui, passa par-dessus ses premières terreurs. Le mariage légitima cette démarche de confiance. Lorsque les premières ivresses du lien matrimonial se furent dissipées avec le bruit des violons, le mari crut toutefois s'apercevoir que sa femme, impatiente de s'émanciper, le reléguerait volontiers au second rang comme une ombre. Tout son génie s'employa dès lors pour contrecarrer ce dessein; ce fut sa pensée des moindres instants, sa fièvre, son obsession, sa manie. Il l'enveloppa de petits soins obséquieux, l'assiégea de craintes qu'elle réfutait, mais en vain: il promettait d'être tranquille, et tremblait de plus belle. Entre eux s'ouvrit une lutte où de part et d'autre ils firent assaut de ruse, elle par crainte, lui par jalousie; et les témoignages d'amour qu'ils se prodiguèrent allèrent jusqu'à l'extravagance; tant et si bien, qu'ils signèrent un acte, entre-vifs, par lequel, surenchérissant sur les sermens de fidélité faits à l'église, ils promettaient que celui des deux qui survivrait à l'autre se donnerait la mort. Un coup d'épingle fournit l'encre de ce contrat; ils signèrent de leur sang. De pareils actes sont aussi nuls devant les tribunaux que devant le cœur humain; on ne cautionne pas la fidélité par des sottises.

Pour ne plus donner l'éveil à Charles, puisqu'il se montrait se chatouilleux sur les moindres manifestations, Marianne essaya de s'acclimater dans ses devoirs; il fut évident pour ceux qui connurent les habitudes de leur intérieur, que cet effort contre nature la conduisait en peu de temps au sublime de la fausseté sans l'acheminer pour cela vers son but. Le détour était trop long pour une nature un peu romanesque; elle devint la dupe et l'esclave de son hypocrisie. Sous une livrée systématique, on s'avilit. Le marasme la gagna; elle se montra négligente au-delà de toute expression, perdit cette fleur de coquetterie, innocent apanage des femmes, assez étranger du reste à celles dont la tête rêve une plume au lieu d'un amant, se rompit tout-à-fait au mensonge, perdit enfin la verve d'esprit dont elle avait donné des preuves; et, parallèlement, toujours indiscrète dans ses propos, elle livra son ménage au ridicule par ses plaintes sans fin et sans prudence à de bonnes amies sur la jalousie de cet homme qui la garrottait et l'étouffait. Parmi les bonnes amies, suivant la diversité des caractères, les unes jasèrent méchamment, et ce fut le plus grand nombre; les autres, qui se crurent très habiles, moralisèrent le mari, qui, sans tenir compte des maximes de liberté dont on cherchait à lui donner le goût, ne serra que plus rudement la courroie du ménage. L'esprit de propriété nous rend tigres. Il fut jaloux des idées qu'elle jetait sur le papier; l'imagination, dit Montaigne, est la folle du logis, et la plume ne vit que de hardiesses; Marianne n'écrivit plus.

Un mal enfante inévitablement un autre mal. Charles se mit au service des fantômes qu'il avait dans l'esprit et perdit sa place pour s'établir en sentinelle autour de sa femme. Les protecteurs l'effrayaient; tous les protecteurs en voulaient à son bien, suivant lui. La misère vint, et, avec la misère, les rudesses qu'elle développe; un enfant leur

amena des embarras sans cimenter ces âmes qui se bles-
saient de plus en plus et cherchaient à s'effacer l'une devant
l'autre. Charles eut moins de ménagemens dans les formes,
quand les soucis l'assiégèrent. Bref, il s'en prit au hasard de
les faire vivre, ne se souciant de rien, pourvu qu'il ne quit-
tât pas sa femme d'une minute. Un homme qui a vécu sait
qu'une infidélité se commet très lestement; et Charles avait
vécu. Qu'une femme ait de l'amour pour un jaloux, cela
même le fait trembler; il se dit qu'elle peut en avoir autant
pour les autres. Les ménages dont il était entouré ne le ras-
suraient d'ailleurs pas; son ambition était d'éviter le sort
commun. Marianne, s'incarcérant elle-même, ajoutait à sa
propre servilité par des maximes de complaisance que le
mari prenait au mot; elle ajoutait des anneaux à sa chaîne.
Un jour, il lui proposa de l'enfermer chez elle à double tour
quand il irait dehors; bien entendu, disait-il, pour qu'on ne
l'importunât pas, puisqu'elle se plaignait des visites; elle
esquiva la proposition, mais non sans peine. Tous deux s'a-
coquinèrent ainsi dans la fatigue du tête-à-tête, avec leur
idée secrète, leur affection mensongère, leur double supplice. Plus de toilette, plus de travail littéraire, plus
d'avenir: la métamorphose était complète, au point de rendre la jalousie même inconcevable. Tout cela ne pouvait
durer: les efforts trop tendus doivent rompre les forces.
Charles étouffait, et avait besoin d'air; il fallut ouvrir un
peu la prison, voir du monde, chercher des liens nouveaux,
des occasions de respirer, des amis, des moyens de vivre.
Les parens de Marianne, anciens selliers enrichis, vinrent
les voir du fond de leur province; cela servit de prétexte. On
parla de leur monter une certain matériel, d'établir un petit
commerce. Les parens étaient des gens trop personnels pour
voir clair dans le ménage de leurs enfans. Marianne et
Charles auraient eu quelques scrupules à s'expliquer devant
eux. On vécut plus au large pendant quelque temps. On
revit les anciens amis; on renoua des relations rompues.
Mais, pour aller doucement dans cette nouvelle phase d'ex-

istence où tous les deux n'entraient pas sans alarme, Marianne, qui tremblait de perdre pied sur le sol en s'y montrant trop à l'aise, fit promettre à Charles qu'il ne la quitterait pas; et, de la sorte, quoiqu'en s'élargissant, leur prison ne fut cependant qu'une prison. A dîner, ils se mettaient chaise contre chaise, pieds sur pieds; où l'on voyait l'un, on découvrait l'autre. Charles répondait pour sa femme; il s'emparait de son bras pour sortir; il résistait aux agaceries des femmes qui lui tendaient la joue de peur que l'on ne prît la liberté d'embrasser Marianne. Elle se formalisait de la moindre vétille afin de le rassurer, et ne disait pas un mot de peur de s'attirer un compliment. Sa servitude affligeait; cette servitude était trop marquée pour ne pas être un calcul. Les imbéciles disaient: —Quel ravissant ménage!... Sur cinquante ménages, il y en a un comme cela; le sacrement n'est qu'une loterie. Avec un pareil jaloux, on doit redouter les antécédens, et quelle femme n'a pas des antécédens! Marianne, avant de connaître Charles, entraînée par le démon épistolaire, avait noué une relation de tête avec un jeune poète; et tous deux, platoniciens mélancoliques, séparés par les circonstances, s'étaient écrit tour à tour des billets-doux à la façon de lettres de Démoustiers, absolument innocentes, assaisonnées de madrigaux. Ce commerce de céladonisme avait duré jusqu'aux environs de la noce; une infidélité du correspondant, ébruitée mal à propos, avait tout rompu; rien de plus exigeant que le céladonisme. Parce qu'il est timide, il se nourrit de susceptibilités inouies. Le dépit, aussi bien que le conseil de la bonne amie, joint au caractère de Marianne, fut certainement pour beaucoup dans le coup de tête du mariage. Une amante colère se jette au cou du premier venu, et les hommes se confient trop à leur mérite pour ne pas s'y tromper. Les lettres existaient encore. L'occasion se présenta de les reprendre et de les anéantir; ce fut au moyen d'une dame qui se chargea de mener la restitution à bonne fin. Marianne reçut effectivement les siennes, et se proposa de les brûler; mais l'amour-propre recule toujours devant le sacrifice de lui-même. Marianne se plut à se relire; c'était le parfum de sa destinée perdue qu'elle se prenait à respirer. Elle ne quittait pas ses lettres, pensant qu'une femme est encore sa meilleure et sa plus sûre cachette; en quoi, la pauvre enfant raisonnait juste, mais oubliait l'imprévu.

Un jour, son mari, prêt à sortir et cherchant je ne sais quelle petite clef qu'il ne trouvait pas, la pria, par impatience, de chercher sur elle-même, ce que naïvement elle fit, en tirant pour cela les papiers mystérieux dont il prit inquiétude, voulant voir aussitôt ce que ce pouvait être. Elle résista; il persista. L'adultère fut la première pensée de Charles; ce fut comme une détonation dans son cerveau. Puis, sur un éclat de colère, dont les amis n'ont jamais bien su toute la portée, elle se réfugia derrière des meubles, où il y eut un corps à corps. La femme ne put se défendre; le mari s'empara du tout. Quand Marianne se vit en face des conséquences d'un mystère où Charles, avec sa pusillanimité conjugale, plongerait les yeux pour la première fois, sans considérer qu'elle allait aggraver les doutes de Charles, elle se releva, courut vers la porte, et le menaça de ne plus remettre les pieds à la maison, de s'enfuir, de se noyer, s'il ne restituait le tout à l'instant. Les lèvres pâles de Marianne, sa voix brève et délibérée, l'ascendant qu'elle prenait enfin quoique infiniment trop tard, tout pétrifia le malheureux, qui redouta d'en apprendre plus qu'il ne pourrait en supporter, et vit bien d'ailleurs qu'il briserait peut-être la chaîne de son esclave. Au jaloux, il faut un esclave. Le jaloux peut être amant, mais l'amour n'est qu'un sentiment de luxe pour la jalousie; le jaloux est avant tout propriétaire. Il rendit les lettres et conjura Marianne de se calmer. Ses yeux troublés n'avaient rien vu de l'écriture, ou plutôt il y avait vu toutes les écritures des gens suspects de faire la cour à sa femme. Restitution faite, il leur fut impossible de se dire un mot de plus, de se regarder, de chercher à se rapatrier. Charles sortit un instant pour se remettre, pour se consulter, pour savoir comment il reviendrait à la charge sur l'explication interrompue. Tout vacillait devant ses yeux; il se croyait devant un autre avenir; et, comme lorsque la générosité devient une nécessité on s'en fait un héroïsme, il se promettait d'être généreux. Il ne devait pas en avoir l'occasion.

Quand il revint, sa femme était disparue, et des débris de papier consumé voltigeaient dans l'âtre. Il essaya de lire ces fragmens consumés, de surprendre à leurs cendres des secrets évanouis au vol de la flamme; et s'interrogeant sur les amans qu'avait pu se donner l'infidèle, il résolut de courir chez ceux qui lui paraissaient devoir mériter la préférence; tout cela sans projet bien arrêté, quoique le doute et le désespoir dussent lui faire enfanter des projets ridicules. Un de ceux qu'il lui plut d'accuser de la séduction, sous ce prétexte qu'en revoyant le monde, Marianne avait effectivement repris un peu de courage pour sa toilette, et que cette circonstance cadrait avec des visites chez le prétendu séducteur; celui-là, disons-nous, dégoûta Charles d'aller plus loin, et de colporter ses soupçons, en coupant court à toute explication sur ce point délicat. Il ne descendit pas à se défendre: la négation n'eût rien prouvé; l'affirmation n'aurait été qu'une ignominie. Même en supposant que le fait fût vrai, il y a de ces choses qu'un lâche seul avoue. Lorsqu'un mari a des certitudes, c'est à lui de se décider; seulement, l'homme qui refusait de s'asseoir sur la selette, blâma cette révélation imprudente, ce colportage indécent des plus petites castilles du ménage, comme très capable, tant de la part de Charles que de la part de Marianne, de les aliéner souverainement l'un à l'autre; c'était se rendre la fable des sots. Au suicide que Charles pressentait avec trop de raison, il opposa constamment son incrédulité; car ces sortes de débats, suivant lui, n'en valaient pas la peine. Il faut d'autres sévices et de plus violents, disait-il.

Le ton de cette entrevue, fier et délibéré, mit notre Charles, plus tard, en verve de soutenir que l'homme qui s'était permis de lui conseiller le silence devait être l'auteur de son infortune. On verra pourquoi. Cette infortune n'était pourtant que la suite trop naturelle d'un ménage posé à faux depuis son origine.

Marianne alors courait de son côté. Une seule amie lui restait de toutes celles que sa réclusion dans le ménage lui avait fait perdre successivement. Elle s'y rendit, et tout porte à croire que ce fut à dessein de la prendre pour conseil ou pour intermédiaire dans cette crise. L'amitié la plus franche a ses momens d'éclipse. Occupée pour ce moment d'une étrangère arrivée depuis la veille, l'amie ne lut pas et ne put pas lire le mot de l'énigme qu'elle avait sous les yeux dans le désordre de sa folle amie; l'évidence lui échappa, elle eût échappé à d'autres. Le spectacle de la joie glace les cœurs affligés; ils voudraient trouver des âmes prêtes à les entendre; et leur préoccupation les rend injustes contre les autres préoccupations. Marianne se retira sans dire le premier mot de son intention, et l'amie, très empressée d'autre part, courut à ses visites. La vie de la maheureuse tenait peut-être à ce fil!... Si Marianne avait eu quelque amant, la terreur l'aurait décidée à lui demander un refuge. L'effroi mène aux résolutions fortes; la peur enfante plus d'actes héroïques que le vrai courage. Elle aurait quitté son mari; elle ne se serait pas noyée, car on épuise alors jusqu'au dernier refuge.

Elle erra jusqu'au soir dans rues; puis, s'armant de résolution, elle alla consulter une femme d'esprit et d'une trempe courageuse, sur ce qu'il fallait hasarder en cette circonstance. Peut-être Marianne spéculait-elle sur une hospitalité que toutefois elle ne demanda pas. Or, les nouvelles s'étaient croisées dans le jour, et cette femme savait tout. Paris fourmille de nouvellistes prompts à faire circuler les événemens. Dans le parcours des conjectures, on avait deviné jusqu'au secret des lettres. «Un mari n'est dangereux que de loin, lui dit la commère; le vôtre est déjà désarmé, prêt à toutes les capitulations; de plus fiers se sont soumis à pis que ce qui vous arrive. Osez donc! frappez un dernier coup, ressaisissez votre pouvoir sur vous-même! Chez lui, vous êtes chez vous; n'abandonnez pas votre maison, on vous blâmerait de prolonger cette absence qui prêterait à des interprétations stupides. Les vétilles d'avant le mariage ne comptent pas, et vous êtes forte de votre innocence. Après un tel éclat, vous devenez libre de vous reconquérir. Il vous a donné sur lui quinte et quatorze; prenez le point. L'exaspération chez les hommes tient de près à leur soumission absolue. Lorsque nous sommes demoiselles, ils se montrent doux et patelins, prompts à s'alarmer d'un caprice, à ramper devant nos moindres rigueurs. On ne doit pas cesser de s'appartenir en leur jurant fidélité. Notre caprice est un frein qu'ils savent subir, d'autant que de leur part nous en subissons bien d'autres. Prenons quelquefois conseil de ce souvenir pour nous créer dans le ménage une sorte d'indépendance.»

Avec ces conseils et d'autres, la dame ramena Marianne sur le chemin de son logis; la croyant persuadée, lui disant de revenir pour aviser sur le reste, lui promettant de tenir cette entrevue secrète, car il le fallait; et toutes deux se quittèrent.

Marianne, cependant, ne rentra pas de la nuit!...

Le lendemain, redoublement de transes, rumeur nouvelle, déchaînement de suppositions, conjectures sans nombre; puis les mensonges obligés! et les gens qui savent bien des choses, mais qui ne les diront pas; et ceux qui ne savent rien du tout, mais qui ne sont pas en peine d'imaginer cent vanteries, cent contes plus sots les uns que les autres. En s'y prenant à propos et de la veille, avec le génie que l'on dépense sur le compte du prochain quand il n'est plus temps, on préviendrait toutes les catastrophes. Mal-

heureusement, la présence d'esprit est boiteuse chez les
jaseurs. Une version curieuse groupa le plus grand nombre
des crédulités contre l'homme qui servait de but principal
aux soupçons de Charles, et vers lequel notre jaloux
dirigeait en ce moment l'artillerie de ses reproches, afin de
ne pas s'en adresser à lui-même. Suivant cette version, les
lettres brûlées étaient de l'impertinent qui n'avait pas
voulu se justifier la veille, qui avait tranché du Robespierre
vis-à-vis de Charles, en le malmenant sur un ton de mora-
liste. Rien ne prouvait le contraire, et voilà comme les
faiseurs d'historiettes procèdent dans ces sortes d'instructions. Mais narrons l'historiette. Il avait séduit Marianne,
disait-on, pour exciter les dépits et réveiller le caprice d'une
infidèle; puis, au prix du sacrifice de Marianne, victime de
ce manège, il s'était réintégré dans ses premières amours;
d'où le désespoir de Marianne, inexplicable sans cela, disait-
on. Ceux qui endurent les avanies n'imaginent pas qu'on se
tue pour un soufflet donné par un mari. Deux jours pleins
furent consommés par les faiseurs d'histoires à deviner et à
mettre en ordre les diverses tactiques de cette scélératesse;
et, l'imagination de ceux-ci venant en aide à l'imagination
de ceux-là, l'on en fit décidément de l'authentique. Le suicide pur et simple, par fierté, par résolution prise de ne pas
rentrer dans un cercle de tortures morales, et de ne plus se
confier à sa propre faiblesse du soin de dompter un jaloux
dont la pauvre enfant s'exagérait les violences; tout cela
n'aurait pas rempli les conditions dramatiques dont on a
besoin dans le vulgaire. Enfin, malgré l'incrédulité de celui
que l'on accusait afin d'avoir le plaisir d'accuser quelqu'un,
le corps de Marianne fut retrouvé sur les grèves de l'île des
Cygnes. D'après l'état du cadavre, elle avait dû se tuer le
soir même de sa disparition du logis conjugal. Par combien
de rêves cette pauvre enfant avait dû passer! Quelle fierté
s'était donc ranimée tout à coup chez elle après avoir ployé
si long-temps? Un amour sans épanchement avait-il con-

tribué à cet acte de délire? Qui sait! Les gens qui chérissent
les malheureux après leur mort, parce que c'est une occasion pathétique de faire preuve de sensibilité, eurent des
déclamations sur tout cela. Dans l'ivresse des clameurs,
Charles, intéressé, comme on pense, à se défendre contre
ses propres remords, accepta ou parut accepter le change. Il
se répandit en menaces contre ce roué, ce séducteur, ce
Robespierre moral, doué de la puissance de conduire les
femmes à se tuer lorsque leurs maris les brutalisaient. Les
curieux se frottaient les mains, et attendaient un nouveau
drame. Il faut des combats de taureaux à la canaille. Ce fut
sur ces entrefaites que la dame à laquelle Marianne s'était
confiée en se trouvant sans amis et sans recours sur le pavé,
vint me confier la circonstance de cette entrevue ignorée de
tous, et une autre circonstance, plus décisive, qui disculpait
de toute participation directe ou indirecte, de toute influence dans ce malheur, l'homme dont il semblait que dès ce
moment les jours fussent menacés. La rouerie renouvelée
de la régence était une fable, une ineptie, un rêve, et cela,
par plusieurs raisons dont je restai le seul dépositaire, et
qu'il ne m'appartient pas de dire; j'en eus les preuves, cela
me suffit. Quand je crus devoir avertir cet homme de se
tenir sur ses gardes, pour qu'il ne devînt pas victime d'une
insulte ou d'un guet-apens, il m'assura qu'il ne craignait ni
l'un ni l'autre, et qu'il se reposait sur la conscience des fau-
teurs véritables de cette sinistre aventure pour dormir en
paix sur ses deux oreilles. Si l'on favorise des crédulités qui
nous disculpent, il n'est pas donné d'aller plus loin. Les
ressentimens factices sont sans conséquence. En effet, la
fable se propagea, mais les menaces tombèrent, et c'est un
exemple entre mille de l'insouciance qu'un homme de sens
doit opposer à des absurdités. Tôt ou tard, elles se réfutent
toutes seules. Aller au-devant des criailleries, c'est recevoir
la loi des esprits subalternes. Mais, d'après cette fidèle
analyse des tortures d'un malheureux couple qui vécut de

divorce et divorça par un suicide, que penser des jugeurs qui s'agenouillent sur une tombe pour graver sur l'épitaphe, avec de fausses larmes, une injure contre la morte, une calomnie contre les vivans!... L'opinion est trop fractionnée par l'isolement des mœurs, trop ignorante, pour avoir dans nos consciences l'autorité d'un tribunal équitable. Entre la version qui purifie et la version qui injurie, l'opinion prendra plus communément la plus accusatrice, à la manière des procureurs du roi et des magistrats. On ne doit, d'après elle, traîner qui que ce soit sur la claie.

Ajoutez à cela que tous les suicides ne sont pas pour être connus, et que la présomption le démontre.

Il suffit, en effet, de citer cet arquebusier du quartier du Roule qu'un dérangement dans ses affaires conduisit à se brûler la cervelle. Il était nuit; la détonation de l'arme, assourdie par d'épaisses murailles, ne fut entendue de personne; mais la bourre du pistolet, après avoir traversé la cervelle, alla s'égarer dans les tentures de l'alcove qui prirent feu. Le quartier dormait. Par hasard un voiturier, qui conduisait un tombereau, donna l'alerte; un cri mit tout le monde sur pied. Sans la rapidité des secours, qui furent d'autant plus actifs que le quartier savait que cet arquebusier possédait chez lui des tonneaux de poudre, on aurait pu le croire victime involontaire de l'explosion effroyable qui serait venue couronner ce drame inconnu. Il avait mis des faux en circulation, par le moyen d'un tiers, comptant y parer avec des rentrées qui firent défaut, et se trouvait à la veille de l'échéance. Le salut du quartier ruina sa famille; on s'abattit sur l'héritage.

N'a-t-on pas retrouvé dans les baignoires Vigier des personnes au fond de l'eau? Parmi les lettres refusées et restées dans les bureaux de la poste, une d'elles, deux ans après, expliqua le secret d'une mort de ce genre, attribuée par les amis et la famille du défunt au sommeil ou à la défaillance, car on ne lui connaissait aucune raison pour se tuer; ce que sa lettre ne démentit que trop amèrement. La famille fut déshonorée par la publicité qui mit la raison de cette mort en évidence. Rien n'est donc plus hasardeux que de conclure; et, s'il faut aller jusqu'au bout, plus d'un assassinat fut si bien déguisé par les assassins que l'on aurait tort de décider contre le nombre de cas où ce déguisement aurait eu lieu avec plus d'habileté. La mort ne dit pas tous ses secrets.

Un médecin vint me consulter un jour sur une mort, dont je lui conseillai (ce qu'il fit) de laisser les causes dans l'ombre, quoiqu'il jugeât nécessaire de soumettre la question qu'une mort pareille soulève trop souvent à l'examen des hommes de cœur et de tête. Il s'en accusait, et je laisse aux consciences délicates à déterminer si cet homme était réellement coupable. Ses scrupules m'occupèrent et m'en donnèrent.

Un soir, à Belleville, où il demeurait, en rentrant par une petite ruelle au fond de laquelle était sa porte, il fut arrêté dans l'ombre par une femme enveloppée dont il ne vit pas la figure, et qui le supplia d'une voix tremblante de l'écouter. A quelque distance, une personne dont il ne discerna pas davantage les traits, se promenait de long en large. Il comprit qu'un cavalier protégeait la démarche de cette dame.

—Monsieur, lui dit-elle, je suis enceinte, et si cela se découvre je suis déshonorée. Ma famille, l'opinion du monde, les gens d'honneur ne me le pardonneront pas. La femme dont j'ai trompé la confiance et l'estime en deviendrait folle, et romprait infailliblement avec son mari. Je ne plaide pas ma cause. Je suis au milieu d'un scandale que ma mort seule empêcherait d'éclater. Je voulais me tuer, on veut que je vive. On m'a dit que vous étiez pitoyable, et cela même m'a persuadé que vous ne seriez pas le complice d'un assassinat sur un enfant, quoique cet enfant ne soit pas encore au monde. Vous voyez qu'il s'agit d'un avortement. Je ne m'abaisserai pas jusqu'à la prière, jusqu'à déguiser ce qui me semble le plus abominable des crimes. J'ai cédé seulement à des supplications en me présentant à vous, car je saurai mourir. J'appelle la mort, et pour cela je n'ai besoin de personne. On fait semblant de se plaire à arroser un jardin; on met pour cela des sabots; on choisit un endroit glissant où l'on va puiser tous les jours, on s'arrange pour disparaître dans le bassin de la source; et les gens disent que c'est un malheur. Jai tout prévu, monsieur. Je voudrais que ce fût demain, j'irais de tout mon cœur. Tout est préparé pour qu'il en soit ainsi. On m'a dit de vous le dire, je vous le dis. C'est à vous de décider s'il y aura deux meurtres ou s'il n'y en aura qu'un. Puisque l'on a obtenu de ma lâcheté le serment que je me soumettrais sans réserve à ce que vous décideriez, prononcez!

«Cette alternative, continua le docteur, m'effraya. La voix de cette femme avait un timbre pur et harmonieux; sa main, que je tenais dans la mienne, était fine et délicate. Son désespoir franc et résolu dénotait une âme distinguée. Mais il s'agissait d'un point sur lequel en effet je me sentais frémir; quoique dans mille cas, dans les accouchemens difficiles, par exemple, quand la question chirurgicale se complique entre le salut de la mère et celui de l'enfant, la politique ou l'humanité tranchent sans scrupule à leur gré sur ces graves questions.

«—Fuyez à l'étranger, lui dis-je.

«—Impossible, me dit-elle d'un ton bref; il n'y faut pas songer.

«—Prenez des précautions habiles.

«—Je n'en puis prendre; je dors dans la même alcove que la femme dont j'ai trahi l'amitié.

«—Vous êtes sa parente?

«—Je ne dois plus vous répondre.

«J'aurais donné le plus pur de mon sang pour éviter à cette femme le suicide ou le crime, ou pour qu'elle pût sortir de ce conflit sans avoir besoin de moi. Je m'accusais de barbarie en reculant devant la complicité d'un meurtre. La lutte fut affreuse. Puis un démon me suggéra qu'on ne se tuait pas pour vouloir mourir; qu'en ôtant aux gens compromis la puissance de faire le mal, on les forçait à se résigner à leurs fautes. Je devinais du luxe dans les broderies qui se jouaient sous ses doigts, et les ressources qu'offre la fortune dans la diction élégante de son discours. On croit devoir moins de pitié aux riches; ma conscience se révoltait contre l'idée d'une séduction récompensée au poids de l'or, quoiqu'on n'eût pas touché ce chapitre, ce qui était une délicatesse de plus et la preuve qu'on estimait mon vrai ca-ractère. Je refusai; mais le refus une fois parti, j'aurais voulu pouvoir le reprendre. La femme s'éloigna rapidement. L'incertitude s'empara de moi et me retint en balance. Le bruit d'un cabriolet m'apprit que je ne pouvais réparer ce que je venais de faire.

«Quinze jours après, les papiers publics m'apportaient la solution de cet effroyable doute. La jeune nièce d'un banquier de Paris, âgée tout au plus de dix-huit ans, pupille chérie de sa tante, qui ne la perdait pas de vue depuis la mort de sa mère, s'était laissée glisser dans une source de la propriété de ses tuteurs, à Villemomble. Ses tuteurs furent inconsolables; la qualité d'oncle excusa sans doute les larmes amères de son séducteur. Mais, moi, j'avais tué la mère en voulant éparger l'enfant.»

Faute de mieux, on le voit, le suicide est le recours suprême contre les maux de la vie privée.

Citerai-je maintenant le trait de cet enfant, enfermé, par la colère de son père, dans un grenier, et qui se laissa choir d'un cinquième au milieu de ses proches, dans un accès de colère frénétique? Citerai-je encore ces malheureux qui, chaque année, s'asphyxient avec leurs enfans pour échapper aux avanies de la misère? Je quitte ce chapitre attristant où le mal qui ronge toutes les classes de la société se met trop énergiquement en relief. Il faut avoir raison avec sobriété.

Parmi les causes des suicides, j'ai compté fort souvent les destitutions de places, les refus de travaux, l'abaissement subit des salaires, par suite de quoi des familles se trouvaient au-dessous des nécessités de leur entretien, d'autant que la plupart vivent au jour le jour, et qu'en général peu de gens sont au niveau de leur revenu.

A l'époque où, dans la maison du roi, l'on réforma les gardes de la prevôté de l'Hôtel, un brave homme fut supprimé, comme tout le reste, et sans plus de cérémonies. Les gouvernemens représentatifs n'y regardent pas de si près; on taille en grand dans les économies, tant pis pour les événemens de détail. Son âge et son peu de protection ne lui permirent pas de se replacer dans le militaire; l'industrie était fermée à son ignorance. Il essaya d'entrer dans l'administration civile; les prétendans, nombreux là comme ailleurs, lui fermèrent cette voie. Il prit un chagrin noir et se suicida. On trouva sur lui une lettre et des renseignemens. Sa femme était une pauvre couturière; ses deux filles, âgées de seize à dix-huit ans, travaillaient avec elle. Tarnau disait «que, ne pouvant plus être utile à sa famille, et qu'obligé de vivre à la charge de sa femme et de ses enfans, vivant à peine du travail de leurs mains, il avait cru devoir s'ôter la vie pour les soulager de ce surcroît de fardeau; qu'il recommandait ses enfans à madame la duchesse d'Angoulême; qu'il espérait de la bonté de cette princesse qu'on aurait pitié de tant de misère.» Je fis un rapport à M. le préfet de police Anglès. On remit une note au vicomte de Montmorency, chevalier d'honneur de Son Altesse Royale; Madame donna des ordres pour qu'une somme de 600 francs fût remise à la famille du malheureux Tarnau. M. Bastien Beaupré, commissaire de police du quartier, fut chargé de la remise de ce bienfait.

Triste ressource sans doute, après une semblable perte; mais comment exiger que la famille royale se charge de tous les malheureux, lorsque tout compte fait, la France, telle qu'elle est, ne pourrait les nourrir. La charité des riches n'y suffirait pas, quand même toute notre nation serait religieuse, ce qui est loin d'être. Le suicide lève le plus fort de la difficulté; l'échafaud, le reste. C'est à la refonte de notre système général d'agriculture et d'industrie qu'il faut demander des revenus et des richesses. On peut facilement proclamer, sur le parchemin, des constitutions, le droit de chaque citoyen à l'éducation, au travail, et surtout au minimum de subsistances. Mais ce n'est pas tout que d'écrire ces souhaits généreux sur le papier, il reste à féconder ces vues libérales sur notre sol par des institutions matérielles et intelligentes. La discipline païenne a jeté des créations magnifiques sur la terre; la liberté moderne, cette fille du Christ, sera-t-elle au-dessous de sa rivale? Qui donc viendra souder ensemble ces deux magnifiques élémens de puissance?...

Pour parvenir à des données certaines sur le suicide, j'avais formé le cadre d'un grand travail.

Je faisais d'abord un extrait analytique et raisonné des procès-verbaux des suicides; ensuite on plaçait sur des tableaux divisés en plusieurs colonnes toutes les particularités caractéristiques: 1° la date de l'événement; 2° le nom de l'individu; 3° son sexe; 4° son état ou profession; 5° s'il était marié, avec ou sans enfans; 6° son genre de mort, ou les moyens dont il s'était servi pour se suicider; dans la septième colonne, je consignais les diverses observations qu'on pouvait tirer du détail des autres colonnes.

Je me borne aux trois années 1820, 1821 et 1824, et à la circonscription de Paris. J'ai cru que ces années suffisaient pour offrir des objets de comparaison sur le nombre et les motifs connus des suicides; j'y joindrai le résumé de ceux qui ont eu lieu depuis 1817 jusqu'à 1824.

Récapitulation du nombre des personnes qui se sont suicidées dans Paris et la banlieue, pendant l'année 1820.

Le nombre des personnes suicidées a été pendant cette année
{ 1er semestre. } 166
{ 2e semestre. } 159 } 325[1]

DONT*
{ vivans............................ 81
{ morts .... 234 }

DU SEXE
{ masculin.......................... 211
{ féminin........................... 114 }

DONT
{ célibataires....................... 157
{ mariés............................ 168 }

GENRE DE MORT.
{
Chutes graves volontaires 37
Strangulation 32
Instrumens tranchans, piquans, etc. 28
Armes à feu .... 46 } 325
Empoisonnemens.................... 14
Asphyxiés { par le charbon 39
{ par l'eau (en s'y jetant)..... 129
}

MOTIFS.
{
Passions amoureuses   20
Maladies, dégoût de la vie, faiblesse et
   aliénation d'esprit, querelles et ...... } 107
   chagrins domestiques.............
Mauvaise conduite, jeu, loterie, débauche,
   ivrognerie .... } 42   } 325
Misère, indigence, pertes de places,
   d'emplois, dérangement d'affaires ..... } 58
Craintes de reproches, de punition 13
Motifs inconnus.................... 85
}

(1) 51 de moins que pendant l'année précédente (1819).

*This category does not add up to the total, 325.—EDS.

Récapitulation du nombre des personnes qui se sont suicidées dans Paris et la banlieue, pendant l'année 1821.

Le nombre des personnes suicidées $\left\{\begin{array}{l} 1^{er} \text{ semestre.} \\ 2^{e} \text{ semestre.} \end{array}\right.$ $\left.\begin{array}{l} 188 \\ 160 \end{array}\right\}$ 348
a été pendant cette année

DONT $\left\{\begin{array}{l} \text{vivans} \dots \dots \dots \dots \dots \dots \dots \dots \\ \text{morts} \dots \dots \dots \dots \dots \dots \dots \dots \end{array}\right.$ $\left.\begin{array}{l} 104 \\ 244 \end{array}\right\}$

DU SEXE $\left\{\begin{array}{l} \text{masculin} \dots \dots \dots \dots \dots \dots \dots \\ \text{féminin} \dots \dots \dots \dots \dots \dots \dots \dots \end{array}\right.$ $\left.\begin{array}{l} 236 \\ 112 \end{array}\right\}$

DONT* $\left\{\begin{array}{l} \text{célibataires} \dots \dots \dots \dots \dots \dots \dots \\ \text{mariés} \dots \dots \dots \dots \dots \dots \dots \dots \dots \end{array}\right.$ $\left.\begin{array}{l} 185 \\ 165 \end{array}\right\}$

GENRE DE MORT.
Chutes graves volontaires	33
Strangulation	38
Instrumens tranchans, piquans, etc.	25
Armes à feu	60
Empoisonnemens	23
Asphyxiés $\left\{\begin{array}{l} \text{par le charbon . . . .} \\ \text{par l'eau (en s'y jetant) . . . . .} \end{array}\right.$	42 / 127

$\left.\begin{array}{}\end{array}\right\}$ 348

MOTIFS.
Passions amoureuses	35
Maladies, dégoût de la vie, faiblesse et aliénation d'esprit, querelles et . . . . . . chagrins domestiques	126
Mauvaise conduite, jeu, loterie, débauche, ivrognerie	43
Misère, indigence, pertes de places, d'emplois, dérangement d'affaires	46
Craintes de reproches, de punition	10
Motifs inconnus	88

$\left.\begin{array}{}\end{array}\right\}$ 348

*This category does not add up to the total, 348.—EDS.

Tableau comparitif du nombre des personnes qui se sont suicidées pendant les années.

1820		et	1821	
1er semestre	166		1er semestre	188
2e semestre	159		2e semestre	160
Total 325			Total 348	

Différence en plus de *vingt-trois*, pendant l'année 1821.

Etat du nombre des individus qui se sont suicidés à Paris et dans la banlieue pendant l'année 1824.

Le nombre en été .... { 1er semestre, 198 / 2e semestre, 173 } de .... 371[1]

Dont... { vivans .... 125 / morts.............. 246 } 371

Du sexe { masculin .... 239 / féminin .... 132 } 371

Dont... { célibataires .... 207 / mariés .... 164 } 371

Genre de mort. {
Chutes graves volontaires 47
Strangulation........................ 38
Instrumens tranchans, piquans, etc. 40
Armes à feu 42
Empoisonnemens...................... 28
Asphyxiés { par le charbon .... 61 / par l'eau (en s'y jetant) .... 115 }
} 371

Motifs. {
Passions amoureuses, querelles et chagrins domestiques.................. 71
Maladies, dégoût de la vie, faiblesse ou aliénation d'esprit 128
Mauvaise conduite, jeu, loterie, crainte de reproches ou de punition 53
Misère, indigence, pertes de places, d'emplois, dérangement d'affaires................ 59
Motifs inconnus...................... 60
} 371

(1) *Dix-neuf de moins* que pendant l'année 1823.

Relevé du nombre des suicides qui ont eu lieu depuis 1817 jusques et compris 1824.

Années.	Vivans.	Morts.	Sexe masculin.	Sexe féminin.	Total
1817	66	285	235	116	351
1818	89	241	192	138	330
1819	105	271	250	126	376
1820	81	244	211	114	325
1821	104	244	236	112	348
1822	102	215	206	111	317
1823	116	274	262	128	390
1824* . . .	125	246	289	132	371
					2,808[1]

(1) Le nombre des suicides a été de 511 en 1826.

Ce tableau offre, comme on voit, un total de 2,808 personnes qui, dans le département de la Seine, ont attenté à leurs jours, ou se sont donné la mort par différens motifs. On y remarquera que le nombre des femmes est beaucoup inférieur à celui des hommes, soit qu'elles aient plus de courage pour soutenir les peines de la vie, plus de résignation, des sentimens plus religieux qui les soutiennent dans ces momens terribles[2]; soit enfin, ce qui paraît plus probable, que le chagrin leur ôte lui-même, en les tuant, la faculté d'en prendre la résolution.

(2) Voyez *le compte rendu du comité de l'exercicse 1825*, imprimé par ordre du préfet de police.

*The male and female suicides do not add up to the total for 1824, 371.—EDS.

MORGUE

J'ai pensé qu'on voudrait savoir à combien s'élève annuellement l'exposition des corps à la Morgue; j'y joindrai le résultat du repêchage, parce que ceux qu'on retire de l'eau ne sont pas tous morts, et que, par conséquent, on ne doit compter dans ceux qu'on expose que les cadavres des premiers.

Résultat du repêchage des noyés pendant plusieurs années.

Années.	DU SEXE		REPÊCHÉS		Total.
	masculin.	féminin.	vivans.	morts.	
1811. . . .	239	69	90	218	308
1812. . . .	280	61	78	263	341
1813. . . .	166	54	64	156	220
1814. . . .	217	78	89	206	295
1815. . . .	238	55	63	230	293
1816. . . .	255	71	105	121	326
1817*. . .	95	85	66	251	317
					2,100

*The male and female retrievals do not add up to the total for 1817, 317.—Eds.

Relevé du nombre des cadavres déposés à la Morgue pendant plusieurs années.

Années.	DU SEXE		TROUVÉS EN		
	masculin.	féminin.	rivière.	voie publique.	Total.
1811. . . .	209	46	192	63	255
1812. . . .	258	70	243	85	328
1813. . . .	198	45	141	102	243
1814. . . .	212	61	183	90	273
1815. . . .	218	61	203	76	279
1816. . . .	222	56	198	80	278
1817. . . .	221	70	224	67	291
					1,947